Anchors for Panic Disorder

A Stability Guide for Living Through Panic Without Losing Your Life

Dr. Cindy H. Carr, D.Min. MACL

The Anchored Series

This book is published by **CHC Connect**.

All views and opinions expressed in this work are those of the author. Any errors or omissions are unintentional.

Printed in the United States of America
First Edition, 2026

ISBN: 978-1-971192-33-8

For permissions or inquiries, contact:

Cindy H. Carr
cindyhcarr@outlook.com
www.cindyhcarr.com

Dedication

To the ones who have learned to fear their own body—and kept showing up anyway.

And to the people who stayed steady: informed, patient, and kind.

About the Anchors Series

The Anchors series exists to help people live steady in the face of mental illness through practical tools, clear language, and compassionate support.

Each diagnosis-specific volume offers a structured set of Anchors (principles + practices) tailored to a particular struggle.

- *Anchors for Bipolar Disorder*
- *Anchors for Major Depressive Disorder*
- *Anchors for PTSD*
- *Anchors for Anxiety*
- *Anchors for ADHD*

Anchors of Support is written for the people who walk alongside someone living with mental illness—family, friends, ministry leaders, and helpers.

Anchors of Faith is the spiritual companion across the whole series. It is designed for readers who want to walk with God day-to-day while also taking mental health seriously as a real clinical reality.

Table of Contents

How to Use This Book

Start with Chapters 1–4 to build your foundation.

These chapters help you separate panic from identity, map your cycle, and build an in-the-moment response so you do not accidentally teach panic that it was right.

Use Chapters 5–7 to retrain the alarm system.

These chapters focus on sensations, safety behaviors, avoidance patterns, and life expansion—including agoraphobia-specific work and practical ladders.

Use Chapters 8–12 to build relapse resistance and a long-term plan.

You will learn what to do when fear returns, how to reduce medical reassurance loops, how to rebuild self-trust, how to ask for support without feeding panic, and how to keep your life open over time (including travel and big dreams).

If you are reading in a hard week, use the Quick Start in the back matter.

Do not try to "understand everything" first. Choose one anchor. Choose one small exposure dose. Reduce one rescue behavior. Repeat within 72 hours.

Chapter 1

You Are Not Your Panic

Anchor 1 - Identity
Name the disorder—and name the hope.

Panic has a way of introducing itself like a narrator. Not as a gentle suggestion, but like a verdict.

It says:

"Something is wrong with you."

"You're not safe."

"You're about to lose control."

"This time is different."

"You can't handle this."

And because panic is physical—because it grips the body—its story can feel like truth.

So we start here with identity. You cannot build stability on a broken identity. If Panic Disorder is allowed to become your name, it quietly takes territory from your life: your errands, your driving, your work confidence, your relationships, your willingness to be alone, your willingness to travel, your willingness to sit in a meeting without scanning for exits.

You are not your panic.

You are a whole person experiencing a treatable condition.

"Name the disorder" means you stop calling panic a character flaw. You stop calling it weakness. You stop calling it "being dramatic." You call it what it is: a real, diagnosable anxiety condition involving panic attacks and, often, the fear of the next attack—plus patterns of avoidance that grow around that fear.

"Name the hope" means you don't rely on vague optimism. You use evidence-based hope: there are proven treatments and proven skills that can shrink panic and expand life. Treatable doesn't mean easy. Treatable means: there is a way through.

Reflection (30 seconds):

• What name has panic tried to give you? (fragile / broken / unsafe / "too much")

• What name are you reclaiming? (learner / steady / rebuilding / supported)

Why panic feels like danger (and why it isn't always)

Here is the core confusion Panic Disorder exploits: panic feels like danger, but panic is often a false alarm—a real body response to a misread signal.

Your body has an alarm system. That is good. But in Panic Disorder, the alarm can become hypersensitive and misfire. This is why panic often centers on the body: your system interprets normal sensations—heart rate changes, breath shifts, dizziness, warmth, tingling, stomach sensations—as threat. And then the fear of those sensations becomes its own fuel.

The problem is rarely the sensation. The problem is the meaning assigned to the sensation.

When your mind says "danger," your body replies with adrenaline. When your body surges with adrenaline, your mind says "See? danger." And the loop tightens.

A brief safety note (because panic can mimic medical emergencies)

Panic symptoms can overlap with medical symptoms. Chest pain, shortness of breath, faintness, and neurological sensations should be evaluated—especially if they are new, severe, different from your usual pattern, or occur with other concerning signs. This book will never ask you to "just assume it's panic" if you haven't been medically evaluated.

A stable approach is:

- Rule out medical causes with a clinician (especially early on).
- Then treat panic as panic—with evidence-based care.

That is not anxiety. That is wisdom.

The identity trap: when symptoms become "self"

Panic Disorder tries to merge with your identity in subtle ways. Instead of "I'm experiencing symptoms," the language turns into:

"I'm not safe alone."

"I can't drive."

"I can't go into stores."

"I can't exercise."

"I can't be in meetings."

"I'm fragile."

"I'm unpredictable."

"I'm broken."

Those sentences feel like identity statements. They are symptom statements. They describe what happens when your nervous system is trained to fear sensations and settings.

So we begin separating you from the symptoms—without shaming you for having them:

You are not your panic.

You are someone who has learned fear responses—and can learn new responses.

A short story (because many people think they are "the only one")

Let's make this concrete. A person has their first panic attack in a grocery store. Their heart races. Their hands tingle. The world feels unreal. They think, "I'm going to pass out." They rush to the car—and feel relief. Their brain records a lesson:

"Grocery store = danger. Car = safety."

The next time they go to the store, their brain tries to protect them. Their body starts scanning and surging earlier. They leave faster. Relief again. Lesson again. Soon they don't go alone. Then they don't go at all. Then they feel ashamed. Then they feel depressed. Then their world is smaller than it used to be.

None of this means they are weak. It means their nervous system learned a rule:

"Escape prevents catastrophe."

This book is about teaching the nervous system a new rule:

"I can have these sensations and still be okay."

Two truths you will hold at the same time

Truth 1: Panic can feel overwhelming.

We will not minimize the experience. Panic can be terrifying. It can include derealization ("this isn't real"), depersonalization ("I'm not real"), trembling, nausea, diarrhea, tingling, heat, cold, numbness, chest tightness, and a sense of doom that feels final.

You don't need to be told, "Calm down." You need a plan.

Truth 2: Panic is treatable—and avoidance makes it stronger.

When you start arranging your life around panic—avoiding places, sensations, activities—your brain learns, "Yes, that thing really is dangerous." Avoidance is understandable. Avoidance is also powerful.

The purpose of the Anchors is to give you a different path: small, repeatable steps that re-open life.

Four myths that keep panic powerful

Myth 1: "If it's panic, it shouldn't feel this physical."

Reality: Panic is physical. It lives in the body.

Myth 2: "If I can't stop it, it must be dangerous."

Reality: Not being able to stop a surge doesn't prove danger. It proves adrenaline is loud.

Myth 3: "I should wait until I'm calm to live my life."

Reality: Recovery is learning to live while fear is present—without letting fear run the steering wheel.

Myth 4: "I need certainty before I can move forward."

Reality: Panic recovery is a tolerance training for uncertainty.

The Anchor practice: language that interrupts the emergency story

Panic hates accurate naming. Borrow this. Keep it simple. Short sentences are easier to access when your nervous system is surging.

The Panic Script (30 seconds):

- "This is a panic response."
- "My body is loud, not dangerous."
- "I don't have to fix this. I can let it peak and fall."
- "I can do one small stabilizing action and stay."

You are not trying to "win" against panic. You are trying to teach your brain the truth.

How to use this book (so it actually changes your life)

Panic Disorder doesn't improve from insight alone. It improves from repeated, compassionate practice.

Here's the method:

- Each chapter gives you one anchor.
- You practice it when you are calm (so you can access it when you are not).
- You practice it during mild anxiety (so your brain learns it works).
- You practice it during surges (so the old pattern loses strength).

If you can't practice perfectly, practice partially. Panic recovery is not all-or-nothing. It's step-by-step.

Mini-practice: treat it like panic (2 minutes)

Write two short lists. If you can't write, say them quietly.

- List A: Signs of danger (rare, but real).
    - Examples: severe new chest pain; signs of stroke; fainting with injury; allergic reaction; unsafe environment; suicidal risk.
- List B: Signs of panic (common, intense, but time-limited).
    - Examples: adrenaline surge; fast heart; tight chest; tingling; dizziness; "I'm not real" feeling; urge to escape; fear of fainting; fear of losing control.

Now write one sentence you will practice:

"My body is having a panic alarm. I will treat it like panic, not danger—unless a clinician tells me otherwise."

Mini-practice: reclaim your name (60 seconds)

Fill in the blanks:

"I am not ____________________ (my panic / my symptoms / my fear).

I am ____________________ (a learner / a parent / a partner / a worker / a creator / a person rebuilding)."

You can choose a different word each day. Identity is not a slogan. Identity is a direction.

What this book will not do (and what it will do)

- This book will not:
  - diagnose you
  - replace therapy or medical care
  - tell you to "just breathe" and act like that solves Panic Disorder
  - shame you for avoidance patterns that grew out of fear
- This book will:
  - give you a framework
  - give you scripts
  - give you thresholds

- build anchors you can repeat when panic tries to run your life
- help you reduce avoidance and regain function step-by-step

The anchor, stated plainly

You are not your panic.

You are a whole person experiencing a treatable condition.

And we are going to build a plan.

Next, in Chapter 2, we map the panic cycle (fear of fear)—because what you can map, you can change.

Anchor Check — Chapter 1 (choose one)

1) Name it (one sentence):

"When this happens, I will call it ________________________ (panic / panic alarm / false alarm), not ________________________ (danger / dying / losing control)."

2) My Panic Script (circle the line you will practice first):

- "This is panic."
- "My body is loud, not dangerous."
- "I can let it peak and fall."
- "I can stay for 60 seconds."

3) One support step (pick one):

- Schedule/attend a clinician visit to rule out medical causes (if you haven't).
- Tell one person: "I'm dealing with panic symptoms and I'm building a plan."
- Write down your top 3 feared sensations (we'll use them later). 1) ______ 2) ______ 3) ______

Endnotes

1. American Psychiatric Association. (2022). Diagnostic and statistical manual of mental disorders (5th ed., text rev.; DSM-5-TR). Author.

2. American Psychiatric Association. (2010). Practice guideline for the treatment of patients with panic disorder (2nd ed.). American Psychiatric Association.

3. National Institute for Health and Care Excellence. (2020). Generalised anxiety disorder and panic disorder in adults: Management (Clinical guideline CG113; updated June 15, 2020). National Institute for Health and Care Excellence.

Chapter 2
Understand the Panic Cycle (Fear of Fear)

Anchor 2: Map the cycle— because what you can map, you can change.

Panic Disorder is not simply "having panic attacks." Many people experience a panic attack at some point in life—during extreme stress, grief, illness, sleep deprivation, caffeine overload, or after a frightening event. A panic attack can be terrifying and still be a one-time occurrence.

What often turns panic into a disorder is what happens next: the fear of panic becomes its own threat. That "fear of fear" can change how you live. It makes you scan your body, scan environments, and rehearse escape routes. It teaches your brain to treat ordinary sensations like warning sirens.

The fear of panic becomes its own threat.

This chapter gives you a map—and maps matter. When panic feels random, it feels powerful. When you can see the pattern, panic loses some of its authority.

A map does not remove fear instantly. But it gives you something panic hates: a plan. And a plan creates a new kind of confidence—not "I'll never feel this," but "I'll know what to do when I feel this."

The core idea: panic is a learning loop

Panic Disorder is maintained by learning. That statement is not blame. It is hope. Your brain learned patterns that made sense in the moment—and because brains can learn, brains can unlearn.

Many people's nervous systems learn a set of rules like these:

- "These sensations mean danger."
- "These places are risky."
- "Escape prevents catastrophe."

Mapping the cycle helps you see where those rules are reinforced—and where new learning can begin.

The panic cycle (the fear-of-fear loop)

Here is the most common loop. Read it slowly and notice where you recognize yourself:

1) Trigger (external or internal)

A trigger can be a place (a store, a bridge, a church, a meeting), a thought ("What if I faint?"), or a sensation (tight chest, dizziness, warm face, an "unreal" feeling).

Sometimes the trigger is subtle: sleep loss, hunger, conflict, hormonal shifts, caffeine, alcohol rebound, being far from home, or a long season of holding it together.

2) Sensation

Your body shifts—often in normal human ways. Heart rate changes. Breathing changes. Muscles tense. You may feel dizziness, tingling, nausea, heat, chills, chest tightness, or a sense of unreality.

In Panic Disorder, the body becomes a "threat detector," so ordinary sensations can feel like alarms.

3) Interpretation (catastrophic meaning)

This is where panic grabs the microphone. The mind assigns a terrifying meaning to the sensation.

Common panic interpretations include:

- "This is a heart attack."
- "I'm going to pass out."
- "I'm going to stop breathing."
- "I'm going to lose control."
- "I'm going to go crazy."
- "I'll embarrass myself and won't escape."

Notice what the interpretation does: it turns discomfort into danger.

4) Alarm response (adrenaline surge)

Your nervous system responds as if the interpretation is true. Adrenaline rises. Breathing may become shallow or fast. Muscles brace. Your body prepares to fight, flee, or freeze.

5) Confirmation

Symptoms intensify, and the brain says:

"See? I told you."

This is why panic can feel like proof. But adrenaline is not proof of danger. It is proof of alarm.

6) Escape / avoidance / safety behaviors

You do something to feel safer—often quickly:

- You leave or step out.
- You sit near exits.
- You call or text someone.
- You avoid being alone.
- You carry items "just in case."
- You check your pulse.

- You avoid exercise.
- You avoid stores, bridges, crowds, meetings.
- You don't travel far from "safe zones."

These behaviors make sense in the moment. They create short-term relief. But long-term they teach the brain a powerful lesson: "Good job. That was dangerous. Avoid again."

7) Anticipatory anxiety (the scanning phase)

Now you fear the next one. You monitor your body. You monitor the room. You brace.

And the scanning creates more sensations, which triggers more catastrophic meaning, which triggers more adrenaline. The loop tightens.

The cycle in one sentence

Trigger → Sensation → Catastrophic meaning → Adrenaline → More sensations → Escape/safety behaviors → Increased fear of fear.

That's the engine. We will interrupt it at multiple points in this book.

Your two fuel sources: interpretation and escape-learning

Panic tends to run on two fuels:

Fuel 1: Catastrophic interpretation — not the sensation itself, but the meaning assigned to it.

Fuel 2: Escape-based learning — the nervous system learns safety from leaving, not from staying. So it never learns the most important sentence:

"I can have this sensation and still be okay."

This is why the most effective panic treatments usually include some form of exposure:

- Exposure to sensations (interoceptive exposure)
- Exposure to places/situations (in-vivo exposure)
- Exposure to uncertainty (behavioral experiments)

We will build this gently. No heroics required—only consistency.

Safety behaviors: the quiet partners of panic

Safety behaviors are anything you do to prevent panic, control sensations, or guarantee escape. Some are obvious. Some are hidden.

Common safety behaviors include:

- Sitting near exits
- Holding water, mints, or "rescue objects"
- Carrying meds "just in case" (even if rarely used)
- Checking pulse/oxygen/heart rhythm repeatedly
- Researching symptoms during panic
- Avoiding caffeine completely because "any increase in heart rate is dangerous"
- Avoiding exercise or sex because heart rate changes feel threatening
- Insisting on reassurance ("Are you sure I'm okay?")
- Driving only with a "safe person"
- Always having an escape route mapped

Safety behaviors are not character flaws. They are understandable responses to fear. But they have a hidden cost: they teach your brain, "You needed this to survive."

So part of recovery is not "stop all safety behaviors now." Part of recovery is reducing them gradually, with kindness, as your confidence grows.

A short example: how safety behaviors keep panic alive

Imagine you go to the store. You feel a small surge of dizziness. Your mind says, "Here it comes." You grip your water bottle, stand near the exit, text someone ("I feel weird"), and leave early.

Relief hits. And your brain records a rule:

"Exit + reassurance + leaving = survival."

Next time, you feel anxious sooner—because the brain is preparing to use the same strategy. And the strategy requires fear to justify it, so panic shows up early.

This is not you "getting worse." This is panic's learning loop doing its job. Recovery is teaching a new ending:

"I stayed, and nothing catastrophic happened."

Mini-practice: find your personal cycle (5 minutes)

Use this template. Write it the way your panic actually happens, not the way you wish it happened.

My common trigger is:

The first sensation I notice is:

The story my mind tells is:

What I do next to cope/escape is:

What it costs me afterward (emotionally or practically) is:

Now write one interruption you are willing to practice (just one):

I will interrupt the cycle by:

Examples of small interruptions (choose one for now):

- "Name it: This is panic."
- "Stay 60 seconds longer than I want to."
- "Let my heart race without checking it."
- "Take one normal breath instead of forcing breathing."

- "Keep my hands on the cart and finish one aisle."
- "Finish one sentence before I escape."

Your first interruption should be small enough to repeat. Panic recovery is not built on a single brave moment—it is built on repeated, moderate moments.

A note about altered states (why it can feel unreal)

Panic can create altered states: derealization ("this isn't real"), depersonalization ("I'm not real"), tunnel vision, shaking, nausea, diarrhea, tingling, hot/cold waves, numbness.

When these happen, the brain understandably says, "This must be serious." But panic can create extreme symptoms without danger. That is the false alarm problem.

We don't respond by arguing with your body. We respond by training your brain:

"I can feel this and still be safe."

What you do after panic matters more than the panic itself

Your brain doesn't learn most from the surge. It learns from what you do next.

If you escape, it learns: "Escape saves me." If you stay (even briefly), it learns: "I can handle this."

This chapter is about shifting the learning.

Evidence-based treatment options (so you know what works)

This book is a self-regulation companion, not a substitute for medical care. But it helps to know what treatments are supported by evidence—and why the anchors are built the way they are.

1) Cognitive Behavioral Therapy (CBT) with exposure

CBT for panic typically targets catastrophic interpretations ("This sensation means danger"), avoidance and safety behaviors, and exposure to sensations and situations (to retrain the alarm system).

This approach has strong research support and is recommended in major clinical guidelines.

2) Exposure-based practice (the core learning mechanism)

Exposure is the "experience ingredient" that teaches your brain: "I can feel this and I don't have to escape." That learning is why Chapters 4–7 are so important.

3) Medication (common options, in general terms)

Many people benefit from medication, especially when panic is frequent or life has become very restricted. Medication decisions should be made with a licensed prescriber.

- SSRIs and SNRIs (often considered first-line options for panic disorder)
- Benzodiazepines (sometimes used short-term; can carry risks such as dependence and can complicate learning for some people)
- Other options may be considered based on your unique history and response

If you take medication, the anchors still matter. Medication can reduce symptom intensity; skills and exposure change the fear-learning loop.

4) Combined treatment

Some people do best with therapy + medication together. Others do well with skills-based therapy alone. What matters most is that you build a plan you can sustain.

5) When professional support is especially important

Consider additional help if you are becoming homebound or nearly homebound; if you have frequent ER/urgent-care visits driven by panic fear; if you have strong suicidal thoughts, severe depression, or substance misuse; or if you feel unsafe, dissociated, or unable to function day-to-day.

Getting help is not failing. It is adding structure to the learning process.

Panic overlaps (a quick clarity box)

Panic can overlap with other conditions. This doesn't mean you have all of them. It simply helps you understand why your experience may feel complex.

- Panic Disorder: panic attacks + fear of fear + avoidance/safety behaviors
- Agoraphobia patterns: fear of being trapped with panic; escape feels hard
- Health anxiety: fear that symptoms mean illness; reassurance loops (see Chapter 9)
- PTSD: panic-like surges linked to trauma cues + avoidance of reminders

- OCD: intrusive thoughts + compulsions to neutralize; reassurance seeking can look similar
- Social anxiety: fear of negative evaluation; panic may occur in social settings
- Depression: low motivation, withdrawal, hopelessness can make practice harder (see weekly plans and Anchor 10)

If you're unsure, a clinician can help clarify diagnosis. For this book, the practical question remains: "What keeps the fear loop going—and what helps retrain it?"

Anchor 2, stated plainly

What I can map, I can change.

In Chapter 3, we build your in-the-moment response skill so you don't accidentally teach panic that it was right. And in Chapter 4, we begin the gentle exposure work that changes panic at its root.

Anchor Check — Chapter 2 (choose one)

1) My cycle (one sentence):

"When ____________________ happens, I feel
____________________, I think
____________________, and I usually
____________________."

2) My chosen interruption (circle one):

- Name it: “This is panic.”
- Stay 60 seconds longer.
- Reduce one safety behavior.
- Finish one small task anyway.
- Let one sensation be there without fixing it.

3) One safety behavior I’m willing to reduce (start tiny):

My safety behavior:

____

My “tiny reduction” step:

____

Endnotes

4. American Psychiatric Association. (2010). Practice guideline for the treatment of patients with panic disorder (2nd ed.). American Psychiatric Association.

5. American Psychiatric Association. (2022). Diagnostic and statistical manual of mental disorders (5th ed., text rev.; DSM-5-TR). American Psychiatric Association.

6. National Institute for Health and Care Excellence. (2020). Generalised anxiety disorder and panic disorder in adults: Management (Clinical guideline CG113; updated June 15, 2020). National Institute for Health and Care Excellence.

Chapter 3
Ride the Wave
(What to Do in the Moment)

Anchor 3: Permission—
Respond with permission, not emergency.

Panic convinces you that you must do something immediately—fix it, stop it, escape it, prevent it. That urgency is part of the disorder. Panic is not only a surge of fear; it is also a surge of "must act now."

And if your only strategy is escape, your brain learns the wrong lesson: "Panic was dangerous. Escape saved me."

The goal is not "no panic." The goal is "no emergency."

This chapter gives you a different lesson to practice—one you can repeat even when you feel shaky:

"I can have a panic surge and stay with myself."

Permission, not emergency

Permission is the opposite of panic-fighting. It means responding to your nervous system as if it is having an alarm—because it is.

When panic rises, you will feel two “scripts” competing inside you. One is permission. One is emergency.

Permission says:

- “My body is having an alarm.”
- “I can let this rise and fall.”
- “I do not have to solve it to be safe.”

Emergency says:

- “This must stop.”
- “I can’t handle this.”
- “I have to escape right now.”

Panic grows when it is treated like an emergency. Panic shrinks when it is treated like a wave.

Your 3-step in-the-moment plan: N.A.M.E. → S.T.A.Y. → R.E.S.E.T.

Most people need something simple enough to remember in a surge. This is the plan we will practice until it becomes familiar:

- N.A.M.E. the moment (what’s happening)
- S.T.A.Y. with one small action (what you do)
- R.E.S.E.T. afterward (what you teach your brain)

This is not a test of toughness. This is a training protocol.

Step 1: N.A.M.E. (what to say inside your mind)

N — Notice the sensation

Name what's happening without drama. Examples:

- "Heart racing."
- "Chest tight."
- "Lightheaded."
- "Tingling."
- "Unreal feeling."
- "Urge to leave."

Notice moves you out of mystery and into observation.

A — Allow it to be there

Allow is not approval. Allow is removing gasoline. Examples:

- "This can be here."
- "I don't have to push it away."
- "I can let the wave move through."

M — Make room (soften the body)

Panic makes the body brace. Softening interrupts the bracing loop. Choose one place to soften:

- Unclench jaw
- Drop shoulders
- Release hands
- Loosen belly
- Plant feet

E — Explain with accuracy

Accuracy is not "positive thinking." Accuracy is treatment. Examples:

- "This is a panic alarm."
- "This is adrenaline, not danger."
- "Uncomfortable is not fatal."
- "This will peak and fall."

Step 2: S.T.A.Y. (what you do with your body)

S — Stay where you are (if safe)

If you can safely stay, stay. If you cannot stay (for safety or driving), you still stay internally: stay with your breath, your feet, your present moment, your values.

Staying teaches the brain: "I can handle this."

T — Take one normal breath

This book will not tell you to "take deep breaths" as the primary solution. Deep breathing can become another safety behavior.

Instead: one normal breath in… and one normal breath out… without forcing. If breathing is your main fear, you may feel tempted to "grab air." The skill is to let breathing happen naturally.

A — Aim at one small action

Pick one tiny action that keeps you connected to life. Examples:

- Keep your hands on the cart and finish one aisle
- Keep walking for 30 more seconds
- Stay seated and read one paragraph
- Finish one sentence before leaving

Y — Yes (the acceptance word)

Yes is the word that ends negotiations. Examples:

- "Yes, my body is scared."
- "Yes, I feel the urge to escape."
- "Yes, I can continue anyway."

Step 3: R.E.S.E.T. (after the wave starts to fall)

What happens after panic matters more than the panic itself. Your brain learns from the ending. So we add a short aftercare routine:

R — Recognize what you did right

- "I stayed with myself."
- "I practiced."
- "I didn't have to be perfect."

E — Evaluate one helpful move

Ask: "What helped even 5%?" Name it so you can repeat it.

S — Say the learning sentence

"I felt ______ and I stayed ______."

This is how you teach your nervous system.

E — Ease back into the next normal thing

Not dramatic. Not avoidance. Just return to a normal action: drink water, send the email, keep shopping, keep walking, keep talking.

T — Try again soon (repetition creates safety)

One brave moment helps. Repeated moderate moments change the brain.

The "do not feed it" list (quick traps that keep panic alive)

If you want a short list to remember in a surge, use this:

Do not feed panic with:

- Repeated body-checking (pulse/oxygen/symptom searching)
- Arguing with the feeling ("This shouldn't be happening")
- Making escape the hero (leaving the moment fear peaks)
- Reassurance loops ("Tell me I'm okay" over and over)
- Instead, feed recovery with:

notice → allow → small action → repeat.

Micro-scripts for common panic moments (portable tools)

Use one of these when you need words fast:

In a store

- "This is a wave. One aisle."
- "Feet on the floor. Hands on the cart."

Driving

- "I will drive to the next planned point."
- "I can feel adrenaline and still steer safely."

At home (nighttime)

- "This is a false alarm. I can let it pass."
- "I don't have to solve tonight. I can ride this."

In a meeting

- "I can be anxious and still listen."
- "One minute. One breath. One sentence."

When derealization hits

- "This is a panic symptom. Not danger."
- "I will orient to the room and stay."
- 5–4–3–2–1: look for 5 things you see, 4 you feel, 3 you hear, 2 you smell, 1 you taste.

Troubleshooting (if the tools "don't work" yet)

This is where many readers get discouraged, so let's normalize it: panic tools don't feel powerful at first. Panic is loud. Learning is quiet.

If you try N.A.M.E. + S.T.A.Y. and still feel awful, that does not mean you failed. It means your body surged—and you practiced anyway.

Here are the most common adjustment points:

- "I can't stay. I leave every time." Make the goal smaller: stay 20 seconds longer than you want to, then 40 seconds, then one minute. Tiny wins are real wins.
- "I keep doing deep breathing and it makes me worse." Switch to "one normal breath" and body softening. Let breathing happen rather than controlling it.
- "My mind keeps screaming catastrophic thoughts." Don't debate thoughts. Label them: "That's the panic story." Return to one small action.
- "I panic about panicking." That is fear of fear. Name it directly: "This is anticipatory panic. I don't have to solve it."

- "It goes away only when I escape." That is the escape-learning loop. You retrain it with repetition: stay a little longer each time, then repeat soon.

A simple daily practice plan (because self-regulation requires repetition)

You don't need a lot of time. You need consistency.

Daily (2 minutes)

- Read your chosen micro-script once.
- Practice one normal breath + soften jaw/shoulders.
- Say: "This is a wave; I can stay."

3 times per week (5 minutes)

- Do one mild "stay" practice (3–4 intensity).
- Examples: stand in a line briefly, sit away from the exit, walk with your heart rate slightly elevated.

After any panic surge (2 minutes)

- Do R.E.S.E.T.
- Write one learning sentence.

If you do these practices, you are teaching your nervous system every week:

“This is not an emergency.”

Anchor 3, stated plainly

I respond with permission, not emergency.

You are training your brain to learn: “I can have a panic surge and stay with myself.”

In Chapter 4, we begin gentle exposure—because avoidance is the fertilizer of panic, and approach is the pathway out.

Anchor Check — Chapter 3 (choose one)

1) My N.A.M.E. accuracy line:

When panic rises, I will say:

2) My one small action:

When panic rises, I will do:

3) My R.E.S.E.T. learning sentence:

I felt ____________________ and I stayed ____________________.

Endnotes

7. American Psychiatric Association. (2010). Practice guideline for the treatment of patients with panic disorder (2nd ed.). American Psychiatric Association.

8. National Institute for Health and Care Excellence. (2020). Generalised anxiety disorder and panic disorder in adults: Management (Clinical guideline CG113; updated June 15, 2020). National Institute for Health and Care Excellence.

Chapter 4
Exposure, the Gentle Way
(Re-teaching Your Brain)

Anchor 4: Approach—
Approach in small steps. Avoidance is the fertilizer of panic.

If you have Panic Disorder, you've probably had this thought: "I understand it's panic… but my body still freaks out." That makes sense.

Panic recovery isn't primarily a logic project. It's a learning project. Your brain learned rules like: "These sensations mean danger," "These places are risky," and "Escape prevents catastrophe."

Exposure is how you teach your brain new information through experience:

- "I can feel this and still be safe."
- "I can stay and the wave will pass."
- "I can go back to life."

Exposure is not punishment. Exposure is not flooding. Exposure is not forcing yourself into terror and hoping it breaks. Done correctly, exposure is structured, compassionate, and repeatable.

Avoidance shrinks the world. Approach re-opens it.

Avoidance is understandable. Avoidance also has a cost. Avoidance gives immediate relief, and that relief is rewarding—so the brain repeats it.

And every time you avoid, your nervous system learns: "Good job. That really was dangerous." Over time, the world shrinks.

Approach teaches the opposite:

"I can do hard things in small steps."

This is the heart of this book: we don't ask you to be fearless. We teach you to be willing—one step at a time.

Two types of exposure (and why most people need both)

Exposure for Panic Disorder usually has two parts:

1) Interoceptive exposure (sensations)

This means practicing the sensations you fear in a safe, controlled way so your brain stops treating them like emergencies.

Examples of feared sensations:

- Rapid heartbeat
- Dizziness/lightheadedness
- Breathlessness feelings
- Chest tightness
- Warmth/flush
- Nausea
- Trembling
- Derealization ("unreal" feeling)

2) In-vivo exposure (places and situations)

This means returning to the places you avoid—gradually, on purpose, with a plan.

Examples:

- Grocery stores
- Highways/bridges
- Waiting in lines
- Being alone at home
- Sitting away from exits
- Elevators

- Meetings
- Movie theaters
- Driving farther from "safe zones"

Interoceptive exposure teaches: "I can handle sensations." In-vivo exposure teaches: "I can handle life." Most people need both because panic often attaches to both body and place.

The exposure rule that matters most: repeat, don't rescue

Exposure works because your brain updates through repetition—not through one heroic event. A simple rule protects you:

Repeat the step. Don't rescue the step.

Rescue includes: leaving right when discomfort rises; using a safety behavior to cut the wave short (checking, reassurance, rushing); or making exposure "perfect" ("I must not feel anxious").

The goal is not zero fear. The goal is new learning:

"I felt fear and I stayed."

The "Goldilocks" zone (how hard should exposure be?)

Exposure should be challenging enough to create learning—but not so overwhelming that you shut down, dissociate, or dread it for days.

Use a simple scale: 0 = calm, 10 = full panic. Aim for exposures in the 3–6 range most of the time. An occasional 7 is okay if you recover quickly and feel supported. We don't build recovery on suffering.

Small steps are not avoidance. Small steps are strategy.

Your exposure ladder: build it like a staircase, not a cliff

You will make two ladders: one for places/situations (in-vivo), and one for sensations (interoceptive).

Step 1: List what you avoid and what you fear

Avoided places/situations (choose 5):

1) ________________________________

2) ________________________________

3) ________________________________

4) ________________________________

5) ________________________________

Feared sensations (choose 5):

1) ____

2) ____

3) ____

4) ____

5) ____

Step 2: Rate each from 0–10

Example ratings: Store alone = 7; Store with a friend = 4; One aisle = 3.

Step 3: Break the big one into small steps

If "drive on the highway" is an 8, you do not start there. You start with steps that create learning without overwhelming you.

Example highway ladder:

- Sit in the car for 3 minutes (2)
- Drive around the block (3)
- Drive on a local road for 10 minutes (4)
- Drive to the highway entrance and back (5)
- One exit on the highway (6)
- Two exits (6–7)
- Full route (8)

Step 4: Add a "stay" dose

Exposure needs a dose: a time or distance target. Dose matters because the brain needs time to update.

Examples:

- Stay in the store 5 minutes
- Stand in line 2 minutes
- Remain in the meeting 10 minutes
- Drive for 12 minutes
- Sit away from the exit for the full agenda item

Step 5: Reduce one safety behavior (not all of them)

If you do exposure while using every safety behavior, your brain may credit the safety behavior—not you. You don't remove everything at once. You remove one small thing.

Examples of "one safety behavior reductions":

- Don't check pulse during the exposure
- Don't sit near the exit this time
- Don't text for reassurance until after the stay time is complete

- Hold water in your bag instead of your hand
- Don't research symptoms until 30 minutes later (delay the compulsion)

Reducing safety behaviors is how you teach the brain:

"I can do this without rescue."

Interoceptive exposure: the body as teacher (done safely)

Important: If you have medical conditions (heart/lung/neurological), pregnancy, or any uncertainty, consult a clinician before sensation exercises.

Interoceptive exposure is not "making yourself panic." It is practicing sensations on purpose in small doses—so they stop being scary.

Common clinician-used exercises (choose only what's safe for you):

- Brisk stepping/jumping jacks for 60 seconds (heart rate)
- Spinning in a chair for 20–30 seconds (dizziness)
- Head between knees then raise (lightheadedness)

- Breathing through a straw briefly (air hunger sensation)
- Breath holding briefly (only if medically cleared)

Your job is not to win. Your job is to learn:

"I can feel this and I don't have to escape."

The exposure session template (portable and repeatable)

Before (1 minute)

- Choose one step (3–6 intensity).
- Choose your dose (time/distance).
- Choose one safety behavior to reduce.
- Write one intention: "I am teaching my brain."

During (the practice)

- Use N.A.M.E. + S.T.A.Y. from Chapter 3.
- Expect sensations to rise and fall.
- Let the wave peak without rushing to the ending.
- If panic spikes, make the goal smaller—not the story bigger.

After (2 minutes)

- Do R.E.S.E.T. from Chapter 3.
- Write your learning sentence: "I felt ______ and I stayed ______."
- Plan the next repetition within days, not weeks.

This is how confidence is built: repetition with meaning.

Troubleshooting (the most common exposure problems)

- "I did exposure and I felt anxious the whole time." That can still be a successful exposure. Success is not "calm." Success is "I stayed and the feared catastrophe did not happen."
- "I did it once and it didn't change anything." One exposure is a data point. Repetition is what changes learning. Repeat the same step several times before moving up.
- "I keep picking steps that are too big." That's normal. Shrink the step until it's in the 3–5 range. Exposure should be doable enough to repeat.
- "I do exposure but I'm secretly rescuing myself." Also normal. Pick one safety

behavior to reduce and make it measurable (e.g., "No pulse checking until after 10 minutes.").

- "I avoid doing exposures because I dread them." Then your first exposure is not a place. Your first exposure is commitment: 2 minutes of planning + 3 minutes of a tiny step. Dread decreases when you prove you can do small steps.

A simple weekly practice plan (because self-regulation requires structure)

You don't need constant therapy to make progress. You need a rhythm.

Weekly plan:

- Choose 2 in-vivo exposures per week (10–20 minutes each).
- Choose 2 interoceptive practices per week (2–5 minutes each).
- Repeat the same steps until they drop 1–2 points on your fear scale.
- Move up one notch only when repetition feels more familiar.

Rule of thumb: Repeat more than you increase.

Anchor 4, stated plainly

Approach is not forcing. Approach is training.

In Chapter 5, we will focus on the fear of sensations more deeply—so you can build confidence with your own physiology and reduce body-scanning and fear spirals.

Anchor Check — Chapter 4 (choose one)

1) My first ladder step (3–4 intensity):

I will practice:

My dose (time/distance):

2) My safety behavior to reduce (choose one):

I will reduce:

My "tiny reduction" step:

3) My learning sentence:

"I felt ____________ and I stayed ______________."

Endnotes

9. American Psychiatric Association. (2010). Practice guideline for the treatment of patients with panic disorder (2nd ed.). American Psychiatric Association.

10. National Institute for Health and Care Excellence. (2020). Generalised anxiety disorder and panic disorder in adults: Management (Clinical guideline CG113; updated June 15, 2020). National Institute for Health and Care Excellence.

11. Papola, D., Ostuzzi, G., Tedeschi, F., Gastaldon, C., Purgato, M., Del Giovane, C., Pompoli, A., Pauley, D., Karyotaki, E., Sijbrandij, M., Furukawa, T. A., Cuijpers, P., & Barbui, C. (2023). CBT treatment delivery formats for panic disorder: A systematic review and network meta-analysis of randomised controlled trials. Psychological Medicine, 53(3), 614–624. https://doi.org/10.1017/S0033291722003683

Chapter 5
The Body as Teacher
(Interoceptive Exposure & Sensation Confidence)

Anchor 5: Body Confidence—
Practice sensations on purpose. Your body is not the enemy.

Panic Disorder often teaches one painful belief: "My body is dangerous." Not in theory—in experience. When your heart races, your breath changes, your stomach drops, or the room feels unreal, your nervous system can treat it like a threat.

So you begin to watch your body like a suspicious stranger: checking, scanning, monitoring, bracing. That makes sense. It is also exhausting.

This chapter gives you a new relationship with your body: not blind trust and not constant control—confidence built through practice.

When panic is in charge, sensations feel like warnings. When recovery is in charge, sensations become data.

You do not have to love the sensations. You only have to learn this sentence:

"I can feel this and still be okay."

What "interoceptive" means (in plain language)

Interoception is your ability to sense internal body signals—heart rate, breathing, warmth, nausea, dizziness, tension, hunger, and so on.

In Panic Disorder, interoception can become threat-focused: you notice sensations quickly and interpret them catastrophically.

Interoceptive exposure is how you retrain that system. You practice the sensations on purpose, in safe doses, until the fear response weakens.

This is not "making yourself panic." This is teaching your brain that sensations are survivable.

The difference between noticing and scanning

This distinction changes everything.

Noticing (helpful)

- "My heart is fast."
- "My chest feels tight."
- "I feel floaty."

Then you return to your task.

Scanning (fuel)

- "Is my heart still fast?"
- "What if it gets worse?"
- "Am I about to faint?"
- "Let me check again."

Scanning is a safety behavior. It keeps the threat story alive. Your goal is not to stop noticing. Your goal is to stop scanning.

Quick rule: Notice once → name it → return to one small action.

Common feared sensations (and what panic usually says they mean)

Below are common sensations and the usual panic interpretation. You do not need to argue with the thought. You only need to label it as "the panic story."

- Heart racing → "heart attack" / "I'll collapse"
- Breathlessness → "I'm suffocating" / "I'll stop breathing"
- Dizziness → "I'll faint" / "I'll lose control"
- Tingling/numbness → "something is wrong neurologically"

- Heat/flush → "I'll pass out" / "everyone will notice"
- Nausea/GI urgency → "I'll embarrass myself"
- Derealization/depersonalization → "I'm losing my mind"

These interpretations are common. They are also trainable. Your goal in this chapter is to build sensation confidence.

The safety foundation (read this once and respect it)

If you have heart or lung conditions, significant neurological conditions, pregnancy, a history of fainting for medical reasons, or you're unsure about your medical status, consult a clinician before doing body-sensation exercises.

Also: if you are currently in an acute medical evaluation phase, pause exposure work until you have clarity.

Exposure is about courage. It is not about ignoring real risk.

Your interoceptive menu (choose 1–2 to practice)

You will not do all of these. You will pick the sensations that matter for your panic pattern.

Choose one exercise that creates a 3–6 intensity level.

A) Heart rate / adrenaline sensations

- Brisk stepping in place for 60 seconds
- Walking up and down stairs for 60 seconds
- Jumping jacks for 30–60 seconds

B) Dizziness / disorientation sensations

- Spin in a chair 20–30 seconds
- Turn in place while focusing on a point, then stop
- Head between knees for 30 seconds, then stand (if safe)

C) Breathlessness / air hunger sensations (use caution)

- Breathe through a straw for 30–60 seconds (to mimic "air hunger")
- Hold a gentle pause after exhale for a few seconds (only if cleared)

D) Trembling / muscle sensations

- Tense your whole body for 20 seconds, then release
- Hold a light wall-sit for 20–30 seconds

E) Heat sensations

- Wear a sweater briefly in a warm room (short, controlled)
- Hold a warm mug and notice flush sensations (mild version)

You are not trying to suffer. You are trying to teach your brain.

How to run a sensation practice (the 6-minute protocol)

If you want a simple routine that works even when you're busy, use this:

Minute 1 — Intention

Say: "I am practicing sensations on purpose so my brain can learn safety."

Minutes 2–3 — Create the sensation

Do one chosen exercise. Stop at your planned dose (don't chase panic).

Minutes 3–5 — Stay with the sensation

Use Chapter 3: N.A.M.E. → S.T.A.Y.

Key rule: Do not rescue. No pulse checking. No reassurance texting. No symptom googling.

Minute 6 — Teach the ending (R.E.S.E.T.)

Write one line: "I felt _________ and I stayed _________." Then return to a normal activity.

This is small. It is also powerful when repeated.

Two important exposure skills: peak and drift

During sensation practice, two things often happen: sensations peak, and then sensations drift down. Your job is to stay long enough to notice drift.

If you stop at the peak every time, your brain learns: "Peak = danger." If you stay long enough to feel even 10% drift, your brain learns: "Peak passes."

We aren't chasing calm. We are chasing learning.

Micro-scripts for sensation fear (short, repeatable)

Heart racing

- "Adrenaline is loud, not lethal."
- "Fast heart is a body skill."

Dizziness

- “Dizzy is scary, not dangerous.”
- “I can stand still and let it pass.”

Breath fear

- “My breathing can happen on its own.”
- “One normal breath.”

Derealization

- “This is a panic symptom.”
- “I will orient and stay.” (5–4–3–2–1 grounding)

Troubleshooting (the most common problems)

- “The exercise triggers a full panic attack.” That can happen. It does not mean you did it wrong. It means your fear system is sensitive. Adjust by cutting the dose in half, choosing a different sensation first (start with a 2–3), practicing with a calmer baseline (not exhausted/caffeinated), and prioritizing “stay with drift” over intensity.
- “I keep checking my body.” That is a safety behavior. Make one rule: “No checking until after 5 minutes.” If you slip, reset—don’t shame.

- "I avoid practicing because I dread it." Then your first practice is commitment, not sensation: 1 minute of planning + 1 minute of a mild exercise. Dread decreases when you prove you can do small steps.

- "Breathing exercises make me worse." Stop trying to control breathing. Return to "one normal breath" and body softening. If breath fear is central, work with a clinician if possible.

- "I feel better only when I distract." Distraction can be useful early, but recovery requires learning. Try attention sharing instead: keep ~30% attention on sensations and ~70% on a small task.

A simple weekly practice plan (sensation confidence)

Option A (minimal)

- 3 days/week: one 6-minute sensation practice

Option B (steady)

- 4 days/week: one 6-minute sensation practice

- 1 day/week: repeat the same practice twice (with rest between)

Rules:

- Repeat the same exercise until it drops 1–2 fear points
- Move up dose slowly
- Reduce one safety behavior at a time

Your nervous system changes through repetition, not intensity.

Anchor 5, stated plainly

My body is not the enemy. It is the classroom.

When you stop treating sensations like emergencies, panic loses a primary power source.

In Chapter 6, we will address anticipatory anxiety—what to do before panic, when you're scanning the future and bracing.

Anchor Check — Chapter 5 (choose one)

1) My primary feared sensation:

2) My chosen interoceptive exercise (3–6 intensity):

3) My "no rescue" rule for practice:

4) My learning sentence (after practice):

"I felt ____________________ and I stayed ____________________."

Endnotes

12. American Psychiatric Association. (2010). Practice guideline for the treatment of patients with panic disorder (2nd ed.). American Psychiatric Association.

13. National Institute for Health and Care Excellence. (2020). Generalised anxiety disorder and panic disorder in adults: Management (Clinical guideline CG113; updated June 15, 2020). National Institute for Health and Care Excellence.

Chapter 6
Before the Wave (Anticipatory Anxiety & Pre-Panic Skills)

Anchor 6: Early Response
Respond early—anticipatory anxiety is panic warming up.

For many people with Panic Disorder, the hardest part is not the panic attack itself. It's the waiting—the scanning, the bracing, the "What if it happens again?" and the sense that panic is always just around the corner.

This is called anticipatory anxiety, and it can shrink your life just as powerfully as panic itself.

This chapter teaches you how to respond before the wave—so panic doesn't get a head start.

Anticipatory anxiety is not intuition. It is fear rehearsal.

Your brain is trying to protect you by imagining danger in advance. But imagining danger trains the same alarm system as real danger. So the goal is not to eliminate anticipation. The goal is to change how you respond to it.

What anticipatory anxiety actually looks like

Anticipatory anxiety often hides behind "reasonable" thoughts:

- "I should prepare, just in case."
- "Let me check how I feel before I go."
- "What if I panic while I'm there?"
- "I'll go, but only if I have an escape plan."
- "I'll see how I feel when the time comes."

These thoughts can feel practical. They are often panic rehearsals. The nervous system does not distinguish well between imagined threat and real threat, so repeated anticipation keeps adrenaline simmering.

The anticipatory cycle

Anticipatory anxiety often follows a familiar loop:

- Upcoming situation (store, drive, meeting, event)
- "What if" thoughts
- Body scanning ("How do I feel right now?")
- Subtle adrenaline release
- Increased sensations

- Increased monitoring
- Decision to avoid, delay, or heavily control

By the time you arrive (or decide not to go), your nervous system is already activated. The work of this chapter is to interrupt this cycle earlier.

Three mistakes that fuel anticipatory anxiety

Mistake 1: Waiting to feel calm before acting

Calm is not the prerequisite for action. Action is what retrains calm.

Mistake 2: Constantly checking your internal state

"How do I feel right now?" becomes a threat question. It teaches your brain to stay alert.

Mistake 3: Over-preparing for escape

Excessive planning and backup plans reinforce the idea that danger is likely. Preparation is not bad; preparation that reinforces fear is.

The early-response toolkit (what to do when anticipation starts)

When you notice anticipatory anxiety, practice responding early—not perfectly. Use this three-part response:

Part 1: Name it accurately

- "This is anticipatory anxiety."
- "This is panic warming up."
- "This is not a signal to stop living."

Naming early reduces escalation.

Part 2: Shift from monitoring to doing

Instead of asking: "How do I feel?" ask: "What is the next small action I can take?"

Action anchors you to the present. Monitoring pulls you into threat mode.

Examples:

- Put on shoes.
- Start the car.
- Walk to the mailbox.
- Open the document.
- Enter the store.

Part 3: Reduce one anticipatory safety behavior

Pick one behavior you usually do before panic and soften it.

Examples:

- Don't check your body before leaving.
- Don't rehearse escape routes mentally.
- Don't text for reassurance until after arrival.
- Don't delay "to see if anxiety passes."

You are teaching your brain:

"I don't need to solve fear before acting."

The "leave anyway" principle

One of the most effective panic-recovery rules is simple:

If you are safe to go—go anyway.

Not recklessly. Not without boundaries. But without waiting for certainty. You are not forcing yourself; you are choosing learning over avoidance.

If you wait for anxiety to disappear, panic stays in charge.

Micro-scripts for anticipatory moments

Use one of these when your mind starts rehearsing fear:

Before leaving home

- "I don't need to feel ready to go."
- "I can take fear with me."

In the car

- "I will drive to the planned point."
- "Anxiety can ride along."

Before an event

- "I don't have to predict the future."
- "I will handle it as it comes."

When scanning your body

- "Scanning feeds panic."
- "Back to my next step."

Troubleshooting (when anticipation feels overwhelming)

- "I panic before I even leave." That's anticipatory panic. Shrink the step: stand by the door, then step outside, then return. Approach breaks anticipation.

- "I cancel at the last minute." Last-minute avoidance is common. Make a rule: once I'm dressed/shoes on, I go for 5 minutes. You can leave after the dose.
- "I overthink for hours beforehand." Contain anticipation: schedule a 5-minute "worry window," then redirect. Do not let fear rehearse all day.
- "I feel relief when I cancel." Relief is the trap. Relief teaches avoidance. Expect relief—and act anyway next time.

A simple anticipatory practice plan

Daily (2 minutes)

- Notice anticipation.
- Name it.
- Do one small action immediately.

Before planned exposures

- Decide the step the day before.
- Decide one safety behavior to reduce.
- Commit to the first 5 minutes regardless of anxiety.

After

- Use R.E.S.E.T. from Chapter 3.
- Write one learning sentence.

Anticipatory anxiety weakens when you stop negotiating with it.

Anchor 6, stated plainly

I respond early—anticipatory anxiety is panic warming up.

When you interrupt panic before it peaks, you reclaim time, energy, and freedom.

In Chapter 7, we will address panic-related avoidance patterns—how to widen your life again without overwhelm.

Anchor Check — Chapter 6 (choose one)

1) My most common anticipatory situation:

2) My early-response script:

"When I notice anticipation, I will say:

3) My one anticipatory safety behavior to reduce:

Endnotes

14. American Psychiatric Association. (2010). Practice guideline for the treatment of patients with panic disorder (2nd ed.). American Psychiatric Association.

15. National Institute for Health and Care Excellence. (2020). Generalised anxiety disorder and panic disorder in adults: Management (Clinical guideline CG113; updated June 15, 2020). National Institute for Health and Care Excellence.

Chapter 7
Make Your World Bigger (Avoidance, Agoraphobia Patterns, and Life Expansion)

Anchor 7: Expansion—
Build a life that's bigger than your fear.

Panic Disorder doesn't only create panic attacks. It can also create a lifestyle: a life organized around "not triggering it," a life organized around "just in case," and a life organized around exits, backups, safe people, safe routes, and safe zones.

That lifestyle makes sense when you are afraid. It is also how Panic Disorder gets stronger—because panic doesn't only fear sensations. It fears being trapped with sensations. So avoidance becomes the nervous system's favorite tool.

This chapter is about reversing that pattern—without overwhelm and without forcing.

Avoidance is not weakness. Avoidance is strategy—just not a strategy that works long-term.

Avoidance reduces anxiety now, but increases anxiety later. So the goal is not to shame avoidance. The goal is to understand it and replace it with expansion.

How avoidance hides (it's not always "not going")

Some people imagine avoidance as staying home. But in Panic Disorder, avoidance can be subtle and "reasonable-looking." Common patterns include:

- Going places only with a "safe person"
- Sitting near exits
- Avoiding lines
- Avoiding driving on certain roads
- Never being far from home
- Avoiding exercise, hot showers, or anything that raises heart rate
- Avoiding certain foods/caffeine because sensations feel dangerous
- Leaving early "before it gets bad"
- Choosing smaller lives (less travel, fewer events, fewer opportunities)

Avoidance isn't only about location. It's about freedom.

Agoraphobia (in plain language): what's actually being feared

Agoraphobia is commonly misunderstood. In Panic Disorder, it is rarely "fear of open spaces." It is often best understood as:

Fear of being trapped with panic and having no perceived way out.

It's not the store. It's "panic in the store with no easy exit." It's not the highway. It's "panic on the highway with no safe pull-off." It's not the theater. It's "panic in the middle of the row while everyone watches."

This matters because treatment must target the real fear: being stuck, being seen, being alone, being far.

The three core agoraphobic fears (the real engine)

Most agoraphobia patterns are driven by one or more of these fears:

1) No escape

"What if panic hits and I can't leave?" This is why lines are harder than aisles, middle seats are harder than aisle seats, bridges/highways are harder than side streets, and meetings can feel harder when you think you "shouldn't" step out.

2) No help

"What if something happens and no one can help me?" This fear often drives staying close to hospitals, needing a safe person, or carrying reassurance objects or devices.

3) Loss of control / public collapse

"What if I panic and lose control in front of people?" This fear often includes shame: "What if I embarrass myself?" "What if I can't hide it?" "What if I can't get out without a scene?"

If you only treat the place but not these fears, agoraphobia stays stronger than it needs to be.

The agoraphobic safety net (what keeps the disorder alive)

Agoraphobia is often maintained by layers of safety—rescue strategies that prevent new learning. Common safety behaviors include:

- Always having a safe person present
- Sitting only near exits
- Leaving early "on a good note"
- Mapping routes and backup routes
- Checking the body before leaving

- Carrying "rescue" objects (water, mints, medications, devices)
- Keeping constant phone contact during outings
- Avoiding being far from home / avoiding being alone outside the home

These behaviors feel reasonable, but there is a hidden cost:

Your brain credits the safety behavior—not your strength.

So recovery includes two targets: approach the place (in-vivo exposure) and reduce the rescue (safety behavior reduction).

Agoraphobia-specific expansion: train "trap tolerance"

Agoraphobia recovery often hinges on one skill:

"I can feel trapped and still be okay."

This is not the same as "I can calm down." It is "I can stay with discomfort without escaping." We call this trap tolerance: the ability to remain in a situation long enough for learning to occur, even when your body urges escape.

Trap tolerance is trained gently—one lever at a time: a little distance, a little duration, a little aloneness, and (for shame-based fear) a little visibility.

The expansion principle: go toward the life you want

A powerful question for panic recovery is:

What would I do if panic wasn't in charge?

Not "what would I do if I never felt anxiety," but "what would I do if I could carry anxiety and still choose my life?" Expansion is value-based. You're not expanding to prove a point. You're expanding to reclaim your life.

Your values list (quick version)

Choose 3–5 values that matter to you. Examples: family, faith, health, freedom, community, creativity, career, travel, friendship, independence.

Write yours:

1) ______________________

2) ______________________

3) ______________________

4) ______________________

5) ______________________

Values help you stay connected to "why" during discomfort.

The "exposure ladder" becomes a "life ladder"

You already learned how to build an exposure ladder. Now we apply it to the life you want. Instead of only listing feared places, list valued activities, then rate them 0–10 and build steps.

Examples of valued activities: drive to my friend's house; shop alone; attend my child's event; go to church; exercise consistently; take a short trip.

Example: "Go to church" (8)

- Drive to the parking lot, sit 5 minutes (3)
- Walk to the entrance, stand 2 minutes (4)
- Attend for 10 minutes, sit near aisle (4–5)
- Attend for 20 minutes, sit mid-row (5–6)
- Stay through one full section (6)
- Full service (7–8)

You are not proving you are fearless. You are teaching your brain you can stay.

Ways to expand (choose the one lever you need most)

You do not do all of these at once. Pick one lever and turn it gently:

- Expand distance: go a little farther from your safe zone (e.g., drive 2 more minutes past your usual boundary).
- Expand duration: stay a little longer in a place (e.g., remain in the store 5 more minutes).
- Expand aloneness: do one small step without a safety person (e.g., one aisle alone, or a short drive alone).
- Expand visibility (for shame-based fear): practice being in public without hiding—sit away from exits, drop "perfectly normal," allow mild anxiety to be seen without rushing out.

Agoraphobia ladders by situation (copy-and-use templates)

Choose one ladder to work first. Repeat before you increase.

A) Driving, highways, bridges (fear of being trapped in motion)

Goal: increase distance and "no quick exit" tolerance.

Example ladder:

- Sit in car 3 minutes (engine off) (2–3)
- Sit in car 5 minutes (engine on) (3)
- Drive around the block once (3–4)
- Drive on a main road 10 minutes (4–5)
- Drive to highway entrance and back (5)
- One exit on highway (6)
- Two exits (6–7)
- Drive over bridge during a non-peak time (6–7)
- Repeat during slightly busier times (7)

Dose rule: decide your turning point before you start. Rescue reduction example: no pulse checking until after the drive ends.

B) Lines, crowds, malls (fear of being stuck + visible)

Goal: increase duration and stay through the urge to leave.

Example ladder:

- Walk into store, browse one aisle, leave (3)
- Stand in a short line for 60 seconds, then exit (4)
- Stand in line until checkout begins (5)
- Complete one full purchase (6)
- Choose a slightly longer line on purpose (6–7)
- Stand in line without checking exit repeatedly (6–7)

Rescue reduction example: hold water in your bag, not in your hand.

C) Public transit / elevators / closed spaces (fear of no escape)

Goal: practice short, contained durations.

Example ladder:

- Stand near elevator; let doors close without entering (3)
- Ride elevator one floor with a planned exit (4–5)

- Ride two floors (5–6)
- Ride during a slightly busier moment (6)
- For transit: ride one stop, exit, regroup (5–6)
- Ride two stops (6–7)

Rescue reduction example: no "scan for exits" more than once (notice once, then do task).

D) Being alone far from home (fear of no help)

Goal: increase aloneness and distance without constant contact.

Example ladder:

- Walk outside alone for 2 minutes (3)
- Drive 5 minutes alone, return (4–5)
- Go into a store alone for one aisle (5)
- Stay in store 10 minutes alone (6)
- Drive 15–20 minutes alone (6–7)
- Spend 30 minutes at a destination alone (7)

Rescue reduction example: delay texting/calling until after the planned dose is complete.

Safe-person dependency: a strength-building taper plan

Many people rely on a safe person after losing ground. That is common—and changeable. Use this taper and stay at each step until it feels more familiar. You are not removing support; you are changing the role of support.

- Companion support: safe person stays with you during the step but does not reassure repeatedly. They coach: "Use your plan."
- Nearby support: safe person is present but not "attached" (waits outside, sits at a nearby table, walks a few steps behind).
- Split-time support: you start alone for a planned dose (1–5 minutes), then meet the person. Increase the alone dose slowly.
- After-only support: you do the step alone, then check in afterward. Support becomes celebration and planning, not rescue.
- Independent with optional support: support is available if needed, but not used routinely. You are the primary source of safety.

Key rule: don't pair "safe person + reassurance + escape" every time. Pair "support + skills + staying."

Shame-based agoraphobia: the visibility protocol

If fear is driven by embarrassment or "public collapse," treat visibility directly. Your goal is not to perform perfectly. Your goal is to stay while being human.

Visibility steps (choose one):

- Sit mid-row instead of near the exit.
- Allow mild symptoms to show (don't over-mask).
- Keep your pace normal rather than rushing to "look okay."
- If you blush/shake/sweat, let it be and keep the step.
- Practice one sentence you can say if needed: "I'm okay—just having a moment."

The learning you're aiming for:

"I can be seen anxious and still be safe."

Agoraphobia micro-exposures (high value, low drama)

These are small practices that target being "stuck," "seen," "alone," or "far." Choose one:

- Stand in a short line and do not check the exit repeatedly.
- Sit in the middle of a row for 5 minutes, then leave on purpose (planned dose).
- Drive one exit farther than planned, then turn around.
- Go somewhere alone but text only after (not during).
- Stay through the peak urge to leave, then wait for 10% drift.

These are not flashy. They are repeatable. That's why they work.

Severe agoraphobia (when the world has become very small)

Some people are homebound or nearly homebound. They rely heavily on one safe person. They may panic at the doorway. If this is you (or your client), you are not broken. You are sensitized—and you can rebuild capacity with tiny steps.

For severe presentations, we use three principles:

Principle 1: Start at the true edge

Your edge may be standing at the front door for 60 seconds, stepping onto the porch for 30 seconds, walking to the mailbox and back, or sitting in the car without driving. That counts. That is exposure.

Principle 2: Build micro-consistency

Do tiny steps daily. Consistency matters more than intensity. A 2-minute exposure repeated daily beats a 60-minute exposure once a month.

Principle 3: Separate "alone" from "unsupported"

Early on, you can practice aloneness without isolation: a safe person waits outside; you go first for 1 minute alone, then join them; you text after completion, not during. This reduces dependence while still feeling supported.

A realistic ladder for severe agoraphobia (example)

This is a model, not a rule. The principle is tiny, repeatable, progressive.

- Week 1 (daily): stand at door 60 seconds; step outside 30 seconds; return and do R.E.S.E.T.
- Week 2 (daily): walk to mailbox 1 time; sit in car 3 minutes (engine off).
- Week 3 (3–5 days): sit in car 5 minutes (engine on); drive around the block once (planned dose).

- Week 4 (2–3 days): drive to a nearby location, stay 3 minutes, return; repeat within 72 hours.

The "minimum effective dose" of expansion

For self-regulation and long-term success, expansions must be repeatable. Choose a step you can do again within 48–72 hours.

One big expansion followed by two weeks of avoidance trains fear. Moderate expansions repeated train confidence.

The 72-hour re-entry rule (protect your progress)

Agoraphobia often grows after a "bad moment" if you retreat for too long. If you leave early, cancel plans, or have a panic spike, re-enter a smaller version of the same situation within 24–72 hours.

Examples: if you left the store in panic, return within 72 hours for one aisle. If you avoided the highway, drive to the on-ramp and back. If you left an event, attend for 10 minutes next time.

Your anti-avoidance rules (simple, realistic)

- Don't wait for perfect readiness. If you're safe, go.
- Do the step, not the whole mountain. One aisle. One exit. One meeting section.

- Stay slightly longer than comfort. Even 30–60 seconds longer teaches new learning.
- Reduce one rescue behavior per week. Not all of them—one measurable change.
- Repeat before you increase. Repetition makes fear shrink.

Micro-scripts for expansion days

Before

- "Today I practice expansion."
- "Fear can come; I'm going anyway."

During

- "One step. One minute."
- "I can do this with anxiety present."
- "I can feel trapped and still be okay."

After

- "I did it. I stayed."
- "Learning happened, even if I felt shaky."

Troubleshooting (common expansion setbacks)

- "I expanded and then had a panic attack. Now I'm scared to try again." This is common. The goal is not "no panic." The goal is "panic doesn't control my choices." Repeat the same step soon at a smaller dose.

- "I expand when I'm brave, then avoid for days." That's the inconsistency trap. Shrink the step so it is repeatable, then schedule repetition.
- "I can only do it if someone comes with me." Use the safe-person taper plan. Start with partial aloneness.
- "I feel ashamed that I can't do what I used to do." Shame fuels avoidance. Replace shame with strategy. You are rebuilding capacity like endurance: gradually and consistently.

A weekly expansion plan (portable and sustainable)

Weekly:

- 2 expansions in your main feared category (store, driving, crowds) — 10–25 minutes each
- 1 aloneness step (small) — 5–10 minutes
- 1 body-based practice (from Chapter 5) — 6 minutes
- Reduce one rescue behavior (one measurable change)

After each expansion: use R.E.S.E.T. and write one learning sentence:

"I felt ______ and I stayed ______."

Track progress by repetition, not perfection.

Anchor 7, stated plainly

I choose expansion—build a life that's bigger than my fear.

In Chapter 8, we strengthen relapse resistance—what to do when panic returns and how to keep your life open over time.

Anchor Check — Chapter 7 (choose one)

1) One valued activity I want to reclaim:

2) My next expansion step (repeatable within 72 hours):

My dose (time/distance):

3) My one rescue behavior to reduce this week:

Endnotes

16. American Psychiatric Association. (2010). Practice guideline for the treatment of patients with panic disorder (2nd ed.). American Psychiatric Association.

17. National Institute for Health and Care Excellence. (2020). Generalised anxiety disorder and panic disorder in adults: Management (Clinical guideline CG113; updated June 15, 2020). National Institute for Health and Care Excellence.

CHAPTER 8
Relapse Resistance
(What to Do When Panic Returns)

Anchor 8: Relapse Resistance—
Expect waves—practice the response, not perfection.

If you recover from Panic Disorder, one thing is almost guaranteed:

At some point, you will feel panic again.

Not because you failed.

Not because recovery was fake.

But because you are human—and your nervous system is capable of alarms.

The goal of this book has never been "never feel panic again."

The goal is this:

Panic does not get to make the rules.

This chapter teaches relapse resistance: how to prevent a spike from becoming a spiral, and how to keep your life open over time.

Relapse resistance begins with a mindset shift:

A panic surge is not a catastrophe.

A panic surge is a practice opportunity.

If you treat panic returning as proof you're back at the beginning, you will panic about panic.

That fear-of-fear can restart the whole cycle.

If you treat panic returning as a wave you already know how to ride, you protect your recovery.

Two kinds of "relapse" (and why this matters)

People use the word relapse to mean many things.

Let's clarify, because clarity reduces fear.

1) A spike

A spike is a temporary return of symptoms—often triggered by stress, illness, hormonal shifts, sleep loss, caffeine, alcohol rebound, or life changes.

A spike does not mean you are back to square one.

A spike means your nervous system is sensitive right now.

2) A slide

A slide happens when a spike leads to avoidance, safety behaviors, and shrinking life again.

The slide is not caused by the panic itself.

The slide is caused by the response to the panic.

Our goal is to prevent the slide.

The relapse fork: the moment choices matter

When panic returns, you hit a fork in the road.

Path A (the slide):

panic → fear → avoidance/rescue → relief → more fear → smaller life

Path B (relapse resistance):

panic → name it → small action → repeat → confidence → open life

You will not always choose Path B perfectly.

But you can choose it often enough to change your life.

The 24-hour rule (a practical relapse prevention principle)

After a panic episode, your nervous system is more likely to want avoidance.

That's normal.

So we use a simple rule:

Within 24–72 hours, repeat a small version of the same situation.

Not as punishment.

As protection.

Example:

If you panicked in the store and left early,

return within a day or two and do a smaller dose:

one aisle, five minutes, with one safety behavior reduced.

This prevents panic from "claiming the territory."

Your relapse plan: the 3-part protocol

When panic returns, use this plan.

Part 1: Stabilize (in the moment)

Use Chapter 3:

N.A.M.E. → S.T.A.Y.

Part 2: Teach the ending (aftercare)

Use R.E.S.E.T.:

- "I stayed with myself."
- "I practiced."
- "I felt fear and it passed."

Part 3: Re-enter (within 24–72 hours)

Repeat a small exposure or expansion step.

Do not let avoidance set a new baseline.

This is how you keep your recovery.

Common relapse triggers (so you don't personalize them)

Relapse spikes often happen during:

- major life stress (grief, conflict, deadlines, caregiving)
- illness or inflammation
- sleep disruption
- hormonal changes
- caffeine increase or alcohol rebound
- medication changes
- travel or schedule disruption
- long periods of "holding it together"

When a spike happens, your brain may say:

"See? It's back. You'll never be free."

That is the panic story.

Not the truth.

The "maintenance anchors" (what keeps gains alive)

Recovery holds when you keep a few practices in rotation.

Maintenance practices (choose 3):

1) One body-based practice per week (Chapter 5)

2) One in-vivo expansion per week (Chapter 7)

3) One safety behavior reduction target per month (tiny)

4) One "anticipatory response" practice per week (Chapter 6)

5) Review your scripts once a week (30 seconds)

This is not a strict program.

It's a rhythm.

Micro-scripts for relapse moments

When panic returns, you need words that protect your progress.

Use one of these:

- “This is a spike, not a reset.”
- “My nervous system is sensitive today.”
- “I know what to do.”
- “I will not make my world smaller.”
- “I will repeat a small step soon.”

Troubleshooting (when relapse feels discouraging)

1) “I’m devastated that it came back.”

That’s understandable.

But devastation is a meaning assignment.

Try this reframe:

“My nervous system had a flare-up. I’m practicing my response.”

2) “I avoided after the panic and now I feel stuck.”

Then you use the smallest re-entry step you can.

The smallest step counts.

One aisle. One exit. One minute. One phone call.

3) "I feel like my confidence is gone."

Confidence is not a feeling.

Confidence is a history of practice.

Rebuild it with repetitions.

4) "I'm ashamed and I'm hiding it."

Shame feeds panic.

Name it to someone safe if possible:

"I had a spike. I'm working my plan."

A simple monthly relapse-resistance plan

Monthly:

- Pick one "territory" you refuse to lose (store, driving, crowds, being alone).
- Do one deliberate repetition exposure in that territory.
- Reduce one small safety behavior related to it.
- Write one page of learning from the month:

  "What did I practice? What helped?"

This keeps your recovery active without needing constant therapy.

Anchor 8, stated plainly

Anchor 8: Expect waves—practice the response, not perfection.

A relapse spike is not the end.

It is a moment to protect what you've built.

In Chapter 9, we will address safety and risk—how to think clearly about medical anxiety, reassurance seeking, and when to seek professional support.

Anchor Check — Chapter 8 (choose one)

1) My relapse script (choose one line):

2) My 24–72 hour re-entry plan:

If I have a panic spike in ____________________, I will repeat a smaller step within 72 hours:

3) One maintenance practice I will keep weekly:

Endnotes

18. American Psychiatric Association. (2010). Practice guideline for the treatment of patients with panic disorder (2nd ed.). American Psychiatric Association.

19. National Institute for Health and Care Excellence. (2020). Generalised anxiety disorder and panic disorder in adults: Management (Clinical guideline CG113; updated June 15, 2020). National Institute for Health and Care Excellence.

Chapter 9
Safety, Certainty, and Medical Fear (When to Reassure, When to Practice)

Anchor 9: Safety and Risk—
Respect real risk—don't let fear invent it.

One of the most confusing parts of Panic Disorder is this question: "What if this time it's real?"

Panic symptoms can closely mimic medical emergencies: chest pain, shortness of breath, dizziness, numbness, heat, and a sense of doom. So it makes sense that many people with panic live in a state of medical uncertainty—never fully trusting their body.

This chapter helps you walk the line between appropriate medical care and panic-driven reassurance seeking, so fear doesn't quietly take over your decision-making.

This anchor matters because panic thrives on ambiguity, and certainty-seeking can quietly become a full-time job. Our goal is not reckless dismissal. Our goal is clear, grounded judgment.

Why panic creates medical fear

Panic attacks activate some of the same systems involved in true medical emergencies: cardiovascular arousal, respiratory changes, neurological sensations, and gastrointestinal urgency.

After enough panic episodes, your threat detector can become overly sensitive. It prefers false alarms to missed danger. This is not weakness. It is a nervous system that learned too well.

The reassurance loop (how medical fear gets reinforced)

Medical reassurance can be helpful. It can also become a trap. The loop often looks like this:

- Sensation appears
- Catastrophic interpretation ("What if this is serious?")
- Medical checking / reassurance seeking
- Temporary relief
- Increased future sensitivity

The relief feels real, but the brain learns:

"I needed reassurance to survive."

So next time, fear arrives faster.

Appropriate care vs panic-driven care

This distinction protects both safety and recovery.

Appropriate medical care

- New, unusual, or clearly different symptoms
- Symptoms with objective red flags
- Symptoms that do not match your panic pattern
- Symptoms that persist or worsen over time
- Guidance from a trusted clinician

Panic-driven care

- Repeated evaluation for the same symptoms
- Urgent care visits that follow panic spikes
- Frequent body checking "just to be sure"
- Repeated testing despite medical reassurance
- Googling symptoms during anxiety

Learning to tell the difference is a core recovery skill.

A grounding decision filter (use this before seeking reassurance)

When fear spikes, ask yourself:

- Is this symptom new or different from my usual panic pattern?
- Did this begin during anxiety, stress, or anticipation?
- Have I been medically evaluated for this before?
- Is my urge coming from fear or from new information?
- What would my trusted clinician advise me to do in this moment?

You do not need perfect certainty. You need reasonable confidence.

The "medical baseline" principle

Many people with panic never feel safe because they never establish a baseline. A medical baseline means: you have had an appropriate medical evaluation, you understand what has been ruled out, and you have a clear plan for future symptoms.

Once a baseline is established, repeated reassurance is rarely helpful. Practice becomes the safer path. If you do not have a baseline, your first step is not exposure—it is clarity.

Working with health anxiety (when panic and illness fear overlap)

Some people experience panic primarily through medical fear. Others develop medical fear after panic episodes. In both cases, fear focuses on the body, attention narrows, and reassurance can start to feel addictive.

A key recovery skill is learning to delay reassurance. Delay does not mean denial. It means: "I will give my nervous system time to settle before deciding."

Common rule: Delay reassurance by 24 hours unless red flags are present.

Often, fear fades—and the brain learns a new lesson.

Safety behaviors that masquerade as responsibility

These behaviors can feel responsible. They are often panic-driven. Examples:

- Checking blood pressure repeatedly
- Monitoring heart rate all day
- Tracking oxygen saturation compulsively
- Avoiding exercise "to protect the heart"
- Restricting activities "until I feel sure"
- Frequent medical searches

These behaviors don't create safety. They create vigilance. Reducing them gently is part of recovery.

How to reduce reassurance safely (step-by-step)

You do not stop reassurance all at once. You reduce it strategically:

- Identify your reassurance habits. What do you do when fear hits—checking, calling, searching, monitoring?
- Choose one delay (e.g., "I will wait 20 minutes before checking" or "I will wait until tomorrow before searching").
- Pair delay with practice: use N.A.M.E. + S.T.A.Y., then return to a small valued action.
- Track learning: write, "I felt fear and I did not seek reassurance—and nothing bad happened."

This is exposure—just internal.

When to absolutely seek medical care (clear exceptions)

This book does not replace medical advice. Seek medical care immediately if:

- Symptoms are sudden, severe, and unlike past panic

- You have neurological deficits (e.g., weakness, slurred speech)
- You have chest pain with exertion that does not resolve
- You have fainting without panic context
- You have symptoms your clinician has told you not to ignore

Clarity protects you. Avoidance protects panic.

A simple safety agreement (useful for clients and readers)

Write this agreement with yourself or with a clinician:

"I will seek medical care when

______________________________.

For symptoms that match my panic pattern, I will practice first for __________ minutes before seeking reassurance."

This removes decision-making from fear.

Anchor 9, stated plainly

I respect real risk—and I don't let fear invent it.

You are allowed to take your health seriously. You are also allowed to stop panic from running your healthcare decisions.

In Chapter 10, we will address identity and self-trust—how to rebuild confidence in yourself after panic has shaken it.

Anchor Check — Chapter 9 (choose one)

1) My most common reassurance behavior:

2) My reassurance delay rule:

3) My medical baseline (if established):

Endnotes

20. American Psychiatric Association. (2010). Practice guideline for the treatment of patients with panic disorder (2nd ed.). American Psychiatric Association.

21. National Institute for Health and Care Excellence. (2020). Generalised anxiety disorder and panic disorder in adults: Management (Clinical guideline CG113; updated June 15, 2020). National Institute for Health and Care Excellence.

Chapter 10
Rebuild Self-Trust
(Confidence After Panic)

Anchor 10: Self-Trust—
Trust is built by evidence—collect it on purpose.

Panic Disorder doesn't only shake the body. It shakes trust—trust in your body, trust in your mind, and trust in your ability to handle life without escape routes.

Even after symptoms improve, many people carry a quiet fear: "What if I can't handle it when it happens?"

This chapter is about rebuilding self-trust—not as a mood, but as a skill. Not as a pep talk, but as a pattern.

Self-trust is not a personality trait. Self-trust is a history.

Panic steals confidence by creating the story, "I am not safe in my own life." The truth is more practical: you are capable, you are learning, and your brain trusts what you repeatedly prove.

Why panic breaks self-trust

Panic often creates experiences of feeling out of control, feeling unreal or disconnected, fearing embarrassment or collapse, and needing rescue to feel safe.

Over time, the nervous system can learn, "I can't handle this." Then even small stressors feel threatening—not because you are weak, but because you are sensitized.

Self-trust is the antidote to sensitization.

Two kinds of confidence (and which one matters)

Many people chase the wrong kind of confidence:

- Comfort confidence: "I feel calm, therefore I can do it."
- Capacity confidence: "I can do it even if I feel anxious."

Panic recovery is built on capacity confidence. Comfort confidence is unreliable. Capacity confidence is trainable.

The self-trust ladder (how to rebuild it in real life)

Self-trust rebuilds the same way agoraphobia improves: through small, repeated proofs. We build a ladder with three rungs:

- I can stay with discomfort (in the moment). This is Chapter 3: N.A.M.E. + S.T.A.Y.
- I can keep my life open (behavioral consistency). This is Chapters 4–7: repeat before you increase.
- I can recover quickly after a setback. This is Chapter 8: a spike is not a reset.

If you strengthen these rungs, trust returns.

The "evidence journal" (your panic-proof confidence builder)

Panic keeps a negative evidence file: "Remember when you panicked in the store?" "Remember when you left the meeting?" We build a new file.

Evidence is not "I felt fine." Evidence is "I felt fear and I stayed."

Use this simple format (30 seconds):

- Today I practiced:
- Fear level (0–10): ________
- What I did anyway:
- What I learned:

Do not write long paragraphs. Just collect proof. Your brain trusts what it can find quickly.

Repairing the "I can't" language (identity restoration)

Panic often turns limitations into identity statements like "I can't drive" or "I can't be alone." Replace "I can't" with "I'm rebuilding."

- "I'm rebuilding my driving range."
- "I'm rebuilding my ability to be alone."
- "I'm rebuilding my tolerance for lines and crowds."

This is not denial. It is accurate language for a learning process.

A note on support: confidence does not mean isolation

Self-trust does not mean doing everything alone. The goal is choice. You can accept support and still build capacity.

Self-trust means: "I can handle myself, even while I'm connected to others."

The shame wound (and why it must be addressed)

Many people with panic carry shame: "I'm embarrassing," "I'm too much," "I shouldn't need help." Shame is not a side issue—it increases sensitization and avoidance.

We replace shame with compassion and strategy:

- Shame says: "I'm broken."
- Strategy says: "I'm training."
- Compassion says: "This is hard, and I'm still doing it."

Micro-scripts for rebuilding self-trust

- "I've handled this before."
- "I know what to do."
- "I can feel fear and still choose."
- "My evidence file is growing."
- "A hard day is not a hard life."

Troubleshooting (when self-trust feels impossible)

- "I don't believe the scripts." You don't need belief—you need repetition. Use scripts as behavior cues, not affirmations.
- "I keep comparing myself to who I used to be." Comparison creates grief. Measure progress by yesterday, not years ago.
- "I had a setback and I feel like a fraud." Setbacks are part of learning. Your identity is someone who responds skillfully.

- “I’m afraid to hope.” Start with a smaller word: willingness. “I am willing to practice.”

A simple weekly self-trust plan

- 2 exposures/expansions (Chapters 4–7)
- 2 sensation practices (Chapter 5) — or 1 if time is tight
- 1 anticipatory response practice (Chapter 6)
- 1 evidence journal review (3 minutes)

Review your last 10 entries and notice: “I stayed. I repeated. I recovered.”

Anchor 10, stated plainly

Trust is built by evidence—collect it on purpose.

Panic doesn’t shrink because you tell yourself you’re okay. It shrinks because you repeatedly prove you can handle it.

In Chapter 11, we will address relationships and support—how to ask for help without feeding reassurance loops.

Anchor Check — Chapter 10 (choose one)

1) My evidence journal entry:

Today I practiced:

Fear level (0–10): ________

What I did anyway:

What I learned:

2) My "I'm rebuilding" statement:

"I'm rebuilding______."

3) One script I will practice this week:

Endnotes

22. American Psychiatric Association. (2010). Practice guideline for the treatment of patients with panic disorder (2nd ed.). American Psychiatric Association.

23. National Institute for Health and Care Excellence. (2020). Generalised anxiety disorder and panic disorder in adults: Management (Clinical guideline CG113; updated June 15, 2020). National Institute for Health and Care Excellence.

Chapter 11
Support Without Feeding Panic (Relationships, Reassurance, and Boundaries)

Anchor 11: Support—
Ask for support that builds strength,
not support that rescues.

Panic Disorder rarely stays contained inside one person. It spills into relationships.

Partners start driving more. Friends start "checking in" constantly. Parents become worried and watchful. Coworkers notice cancellations. Children sense the tension.

Support matters. But certain kinds of support—especially repeated reassurance and last-minute rescue—can accidentally strengthen panic.

This chapter shows you how to build support that helps recovery: support that increases capacity, not dependence.

Rescue feels loving. It also teaches panic the wrong lesson: "You cannot handle this."

Strength-building support teaches a different lesson: "You can handle this—and I can be with you while you learn."

This chapter is for the person with panic, the people who love them, and clinicians helping families coordinate support.

The two types of help (and why the difference matters)

Type 1: Rescue help

Rescue help removes discomfort quickly. It often includes:

- Repeated reassurance ("You're fine, you're fine")
- Leaving early every time anxiety rises
- Doing the feared tasks for the person
- Constant availability "just in case"
- Immediate problem-solving for every symptom

Rescue help reduces anxiety now. But it increases fear later.

Type 2: Coaching help

Coaching help supports the person while they practice skills. It includes:

- Helping plan exposures
- Staying present without taking over
- Reminding of scripts and anchors
- Celebrating repetition, not perfection
- Supporting boundaries around reassurance

Coaching help builds capacity.

A key line for loved ones:

"I'm here. I believe you can handle this. Let's use your plan."

Why strength-building support works (the empowering, science-based reason)

When panic has taken a lot—travel plans, independence, spontaneity, dreams—it's natural for loved ones to want to protect you from further pain. Rescue can reduce suffering in the short term.

But here is the truth that changes recovery: your nervous system regains confidence through lived evidence of capability—not through protection from discomfort.

Fear systems update through experience. One key mechanism is prediction error: "I expected danger or collapse—and it didn't happen."

For that update to occur, the person has to be the one who stays long enough for new learning to register.

If someone else rescues (drives instead, exits early, answers the reassurance loop, fixes the moment), the brain does not store "I survived." It stores "I was saved."

This is why rescue can reduce anxiety now but increase fragility later. And why strength-building support allows discomfort now but builds freedom later.

Strength-building support sends three signals:

- "This feeling is tolerable."
- "You are capable of staying."
- "I believe in your capacity, not your fear."

One of the most empowering supporter messages is:

"I believe in your ability to learn—not in your need to be rescued."

Supporter anxiety (the hidden driver of rescue)

Many supporters rescue because they can't tolerate seeing suffering. This is not selfish. It is nervous-system contagion.

When a supporter's anxiety rises, they often reassure repeatedly, push for escape, argue with fear, or over-solve ("Let's fix this right now").

If you are the supporter, your first job is not fixing the person. Your first job is regulating yourself so you can coach instead of rescue.

Supporter self-regulation (60 seconds)

- Feet on floor.
- Exhale slowly (not forced breathing—just a longer exhale).
- Name your role: "Coach, not rescuer."
- Say to yourself: "Discomfort is not danger."
- Choose one helpful line and repeat it (see scripts below).

This calm presence is not passive. It is powerful.

Reassurance seeking: why it's so tempting (and so sticky)

Reassurance is one of panic's favorite safety behaviors because it works instantly—briefly.

Reassurance can sound like:

- "Do you think I'm okay?"

- "Do you think I'm having a heart attack?"
- "Are you sure I won't faint?"
- "Will you stay on the phone with me?"

The problem is not asking once. The problem is the loop. When reassurance becomes repeated, it trains dependence: "I can feel safe only when someone else confirms it."

So we don't ban reassurance. We structure it.

The reassurance agreement (a simple boundary that helps recovery)

If you live with someone or have a close support person, create a shared agreement. For example:

- One reassurance statement is allowed.
- After that, we return to the plan.
- If reassurance is requested again, the supporter repeats the same line (no new reassurance).
- The person practices for a set time before asking again.

Supporter script:

- "I hear you. This feels scary."
- "We already answered that."
- "Now we practice your plan for 10 minutes."

This is kind and firm. It protects recovery.

A reassurance delay ladder (how to reduce reassurance safely)

If reassurance is a strong habit, reduce it like exposure: gradually. Choose a starting delay that is challenging-but-doable, then move up in steps as you succeed.

Example delay ladder:

- Delay reassurance/checking by 5 minutes
- Then 10 minutes
- Then 20 minutes
- Then 30 minutes
- Then 60 minutes
- Then "after the planned exposure dose is complete"
- Then "next day unless red flags exist"

What to do during the delay:

- Use N.A.M.E. + S.T.A.Y.
- Do one small valued action (not rumination).
- Repeat one script: "I can handle uncertainty for ___ minutes."

What to ask for instead of reassurance

People often ask for reassurance because they don't know what else to ask for. Here are better asks:

- "Can you remind me of my N.A.M.E. line?"
- "Can you stay with me for 10 minutes while I practice staying?"
- "Can you walk with me while I do one exposure step?"
- "Can we plan my next ladder step together?"
- "Can you celebrate with me after I do the thing?"

These requests build strength.

The support ladder (reducing dependence without isolation)

Many people need support early in recovery. That's normal. The goal is not immediate independence. The goal is gradual capacity.

Use a support ladder:

- Level 1: Full support (early phase) — supporter is present during the feared task.
- Level 2: Nearby support — supporter is present but not attached (waits outside, sits nearby, walks a few steps behind).

- Level 3: Split-time support — you start alone for a planned dose (1–10 minutes), then meet the person.
- Level 4: After-only support — you do the task alone, then check in afterward.
- Level 5: Independent with optional support — support is available if needed, but not used routinely.

This ladder reduces dependence while maintaining connection.

How to talk about panic without making it the whole relationship

When panic becomes the main topic, life shrinks again. So we build a healthy structure:

- Have a brief "panic check-in" time (10 minutes).
- Outside that time, focus on life topics.
- Celebrate practice and values.
- Do not make every day an anxiety debrief.

For couples and families, schedule one weekly "recovery meeting" (15 minutes):

- What did we practice?
- What helped?

- What rescue happened?
- What small reduction will we try next week?

Short meetings prevent long spirals.

Support for big dreams (travel, freedom, future plans)

When panic shrinks dreams, supporters often get cautious: "Let's not push it." But dreams don't return through waiting. Dreams return through training.

Strength-building travel support looks like:

- Planning exposures before the trip (not avoiding the trip)
- Agreeing on a role: coach, not rescuer
- Creating an "if panic hits" plan (not a "prevent panic at all costs" plan)
- Celebrating repetition and flexibility

A powerful line for travel readiness:

"We're not trying to control fear. We're practicing how you respond to fear."

If panic hits during travel:

- Supporter: “I’m here. Use your plan. Stay for the agreed time.”
- Person: practices S.T.A.Y. and completes a small dose (even if shortened).
- Re-enter within 24–72 hours with a smaller step (don’t let travel become ‘danger territory’).

Boundaries with kindness (for supporters)

Supporters often burn out because they become the nervous system for the person with panic. If you are a supporter, you are allowed to set limits.

Useful boundary scripts:

- “I love you. I can stay with you for 10 minutes, then we’ll use your skills.”
- “I won’t answer the same reassurance question repeatedly, but I will help you practice.”
- “I can support your exposure plan, but I can’t help you avoid.”
- “Let’s do the next small step together.”

Boundaries are not abandonment. Boundaries are recovery tools.

Troubleshooting (common relationship problems)

- "My partner/family gets frustrated with my anxiety." Frustration is common when people feel helpless. Give them a role: coach, not rescuer. Use the agreement. Keep it structured.
- "My loved ones reassure me constantly because they can't stand seeing me scared." That is their anxiety. Teach the supporter the 60-second reset and scripts. Reassurance feels kind now, but it strengthens panic later.
- "I feel guilty asking for help." Guilt often comes from shame. Replace guilt with clarity: "I'm asking for coaching support so I can rebuild independence."
- "I'm alone and I don't have support." You can still build a support structure: therapist (if possible), support group, trusted friend check-ins after exposures, self-coaching using this book, and crisis resources if safety is a concern.

Support doesn't have to be constant to be meaningful.

Supporter Cheat Sheet (one-page, copy and share)

What helps (coach)

- Validate the feeling: "That's scary."
- Name the pattern: "This is panic warming up."
- Return to the plan: "Use N.A.M.E. + S.T.A.Y."
- Hold the dose: "Let's stay for 5 more minutes."
- Praise effort: "You stayed. That's training."

What harms (rescue)

- Repeating reassurance endlessly
- Arguing with symptoms ("Stop it. You're fine.")
- Forcing exposure too big too fast
- Taking over tasks the person can practice
- Making avoidance the default plan

Best supporter scripts

- "I'm here. I believe you can handle this."
- "We already answered that. Now we practice."
- "One step. One minute."
- "Let the wave pass. Stay with it."
- "We can leave after the planned dose."

A simple support practice plan

If you have a supporter

- Choose one exposure per week to do with coaching support.
- Choose one exposure per week to do alone.
- Use the reassurance agreement + delay ladder.
- Reduce one rescue behavior weekly (measurable).
- Celebrate repetition.

If you don't have a supporter

- Choose one check-in person (even weekly).
- Use the evidence journal (Chapter 10).
- Use scripts and R.E.S.E.T. after each practice.

Anchor 11, stated plainly

Support that builds strength makes your world bigger. It doesn't shrink it around fear.

In Chapter 12, we pull the anchors together into a long-term plan—how to keep practicing, how to handle setbacks, and how to live a life that stays open.

Anchor Check — Chapter 11 (choose one)

1) My support request (non-reassurance):

Instead of asking "Are you sure I'm okay?" I will ask:

2) Our reassurance agreement line:

Supporter will say:

3) My reassurance delay (start here):

I will delay reassurance/checking by ______ minutes and practice during the delay.

4) My next support ladder step:

I'm moving from Level ____ to Level ____ by practicing:

Endnotes

24. American Psychiatric Association. (2010). Practice guideline for the treatment of patients with panic disorder (2nd ed.). American Psychiatric Association.

25. National Institute for Health and Care Excellence. (2020). Generalised anxiety disorder and panic disorder in adults: Management (Clinical guideline CG113; updated June 15, 2020). National Institute for Health and Care Excellence.

Chapter 12
Living Anchored (Your Long-Term Plan for an Open Life)

Anchor 12: Integration—
Keep your life open. Practice is how freedom stays.

This final chapter is not about "graduating" from panic work. It's about living anchored.

An anchored life is not a panic-free life. It is a life where panic no longer decides where you go, what you attempt, who you become, or what you hope for.

This chapter helps you turn everything you've learned into a long-term way of living—one that remains flexible, realistic, and resilient.

Panic recovery is not a finish line. It is a skill set.

And skills stay strong through use.

From treatment to life practice (the shift that matters)

Early in recovery, practice can feel like "treatment": exposure exercises, scripts, plans, and tracking progress.

Later, practice becomes integrated into life. You stop asking, "Am I doing my panic work?" and you start living: "I'm choosing an open life."

The goal of this chapter is to help you make that shift.

The Anchors as a living system (not a checklist)

These anchors are not steps you complete once. They are tools you return to as needed. You will use different anchors at different times:

- Anchor 2 when panic feels confusing
- Anchor 3 when panic hits in the moment
- Anchor 4–7 when avoidance creeps back
- Anchor 8 when fear returns after progress
- Anchor 9 when certainty-seeking flares
- Anchor 10 when self-trust feels shaky
- Anchor 11 when relationships need adjustment

This flexibility is strength.

Your "open life" definition (make it personal)

An open life is not someone else's life. It's yours.

Ask yourself: If panic were not in charge, how would my life look in these areas?

- Movement and travel
- Relationships and connection
- Work or purpose
- Rest and health
- Play, curiosity, creativity

Write one sentence for each area. Not goals—directions. Example: "I move freely, even when anxious." "I travel with preparation, not avoidance." "I stay connected instead of shrinking."

Movement and travel:

Relationships and connection:

Work or purpose:

Rest and health:

Play, curiosity, creativity:

The 80/20 rule of maintenance

You do not need to practice everything all the time. Most long-term success comes from a few consistent habits.

Choose your maintenance anchors (3–4 total):

- One exposure or expansion per week (Chapters 4–7)
- One body-based practice per week (Chapter 5)
- One anticipatory response practice per week (Chapter 6)
- One reassurance/safety behavior check-in (Chapters 9 and 11)

This is enough to keep the system flexible.

The difference between a lapse and a slide (revisited)

A lapse

- A bad day
- A panic spike
- A canceled plan
- A week of avoidance

A slide

- Panic starts making rules again
- Life steadily shrinks
- Avoidance feels justified and permanent

Lapses are normal. Slides are preventable.

Your job is not to avoid lapses. Your job is to interrupt slides early.

Your personal early-warning signs

Everyone has signals that fear is taking over again. Common signs include:

- Increased body scanning
- More reassurance seeking
- More planning "just in case"
- Canceling things earlier
- Telling yourself "now is not the time"
- Needing a safe person more often
- Shrinking distance from home again

Write your top three:

1)

____

2)

____

3)

____

These signs are not failures. They are cues to return to practice.

Your return-to-anchor plan

When you notice early-warning signs, respond quickly and gently:

- Pick one anchor to return to.
- Pick one small action.
- Repeat it within 72 hours.

Example: "I'm avoiding driving again. I'll return to Anchor 7 and do one short drive tomorrow."

The 72-hour rule (a simple maintenance safeguard)

If you cancel, escape early, or avoid something important because of panic, re-enter a smaller version of it within 24–72 hours.

This is not punishment. It is prevention. The goal is to prevent panic from claiming territory.

Keeping dreams alive (especially the big ones)

Many people stop dreaming after panic takes a lot. Dreaming feels risky. But recovery is not just about symptom reduction. It is about restoring possibility.

If travel, independence, or adventure matter to you: you do not prepare by waiting for fear to disappear. You prepare by practicing flexibility and recovery.

You don't wait until you're fearless. You travel when you're practiced.

Travel & Big Dreams Toolkit (practical, step-by-step)

Travel can be one of the most meaningful expansion goals. It also brings multiple triggers: distance, uncertainty, crowds, time pressure, bodily sensations, and "no quick exit" moments.

This toolkit helps you build travel readiness without turning travel into a test.

1) Define what "travel" means for you

Travel is not one thing. Choose your current target:

- A day trip 30–60 minutes away
- A weekend trip
- Flying
- A road trip
- Public transit
- Hotels
- Being far from medical reassurance

My travel goal:

2) Identify your travel fear profile

Common travel fear profiles:

- "No escape" fears (planes, highways, elevators, crowds)
- "No help" fears (far from hospitals, being alone)
- "Body fear" (heart, breath, dizziness, GI urgency)
- "Visibility/shame" (panic in public)

- "Uncertainty fear" (not knowing what will happen)

Circle your top two: No escape / No help / Body fear / Visibility / Uncertainty

3) Build a travel ladder (not a travel leap)

Use the same approach as Chapter 7: distance, duration, aloneness, visibility—one lever at a time.

Example ladders (choose one):

A) Road trip ladder

- Drive 10 minutes from home and return (4)
- Drive 20 minutes and stay 10 minutes at destination (5)
- Drive 30 minutes and eat/drink there (6)
- Drive 45 minutes with one planned stop (6–7)
- Drive 60 minutes to a destination and stay 60 minutes (7)
- Repeat the same trip two times before increasing distance

B) Hotel ladder

- Walk into a hotel lobby for 10 minutes (4–5)
- Sit in the lobby for 20 minutes (5–6)

- Check in and ride elevator once (6)
- Stay one hour in a hotel room (6–7)
- Spend one night locally (7–8)
- Repeat before traveling farther

C) Airport/flight ladder (if flying is a goal)

- Go to the airport and stay 20 minutes (5–6)
- Walk through busy areas; practice staying (6)
- Sit at a gate area for 30 minutes (6–7)
- Do a short flight with planned coping rules (7–8)
- Repeat short flights before longer flights

Note: flying exposures often work best with a clinician if fear is severe. But the principles are the same: stay, repeat, reduce rescue.

4) The travel rules (so preparation doesn't become avoidance)

Helpful preparation is practical. Fear-based preparation is control-seeking.

Use these travel rules:

- Make a plan, then stop planning.
- Pack practical items—not endless rescue items.

- Choose one anchor to prioritize if panic hits (usually Anchor 3 or 7).
- Reduce one safety behavior on purpose (tiny).
- Expect anxiety. Do not treat it as a stop sign.

Simple rule: "Prepare like a person, not like a panic disorder."

5) An "If panic hits" travel plan (short and usable)

Save this as a note on your phone:

- Name it: "This is panic."
- Stay for the agreed dose (5–10 minutes minimum if safe).
- Share attention: 30% sensations, 70% task.
- Reduce rescue: no repeated reassurance, no compulsive checking.
- Reset afterward: "I stayed. I practiced. It passed."
- Re-enter within 72 hours with a smaller step if I retreated.

This is how you keep travel from becoming "danger territory."

6) Support roles during travel (coach, not rescuer)

If you travel with someone, decide their role in advance.

Supporter role:

- Validate: “That’s scary.”
- Coach: “Use your plan.”
- Hold the dose: “We can adjust after 10 minutes.”
- Do not reassure endlessly.
- Do not make escape the default.

This is strength-building support (Chapter 11).

7) Post-travel learning (how to store success)

Your brain forgets progress quickly when fear is loud. So you store learning intentionally. After a travel practice, write:

What I did:

What was hard:

How I stayed:

What I learned:

This creates the evidence file (Chapter 10).

A realistic long-term exposure philosophy

You don't "finish" exposure. You change your relationship to it.

Exposure becomes: choosing life even when anxious; letting sensations come and go; staying when leaving feels tempting; returning after hard days; building a lifestyle that keeps your world open.

This is not work you dread. This is how freedom stays alive.

Your panic-proof identity

Over time, a new identity forms: "I am someone who can handle fear." Not "I never panic," but: "I know what to do." "I recover quickly." "I keep my life open."

That identity is the strongest protection against relapse.

A letter to your future self (optional but powerful)

Write this now—before you need it:

"Dear Future Me,

If panic shows up again, remember:

____

____

____

The steps I take when fear returns are:

____

____

What matters to me is:

____

Signed,

Me—when I was practicing."

Read this letter when fear tries to convince you you've lost everything.

Anchor 12, stated plainly

Panic does not get the final word. You do.

Anchor Check — Chapter 12

1) My early-warning signs:

2) My return-to-anchor plan:

When I notice ____________________, I will return to Anchor ____ and practice:

3) My travel or "big dream" ladder first step:

4) My "open life" sentence:

Endnotes

26. American Psychiatric Association. (2010). Practice guideline for the treatment of patients with panic disorder (2nd ed.). American Psychiatric Association.

27. National Institute for Health and Care Excellence. (2020). Generalised anxiety disorder and panic disorder in adults: Management (Clinical guideline CG113; updated June 15, 2020). National Institute for Health and Care Excellence.

Anchors at A Glance

Core Anchor 1 — Identity

"I am not my panic, and I do not make life decisions inside a panic spiral."

Protects: Shame, hopelessness, identity collapse, 'I can't' conclusions made in fear.

Why this matters in panic: Panic can feel like a verdict about who you are. This anchor separates symptoms from self so recovery can be built on capacity, not fear.

Core Anchor 2 — Map (Fear-of-Fear Cycle)

"What I can map, I can change."

Protects: Feeling blindsided, 'out of nowhere' panic, confusion that fuels avoidance.

Why this matters in panic: Panic disorder is maintained by a predictable learning loop (trigger → sensation → meaning → adrenaline → escape). Mapping the loop shows where to interrupt it.

Core Anchor 3 — Permission (No Emergency)

“I respond with permission, not emergency.”

Protects: Panic-fighting, escalation, impulsive escape that reinforces fear.

Why this matters in panic: The core skill is learning that panic is a wave: loud, temporary, and survivable. Treating it as non-emergency retrains the alarm system.

Core Anchor 4 — Approach

“I approach in small steps—avoidance is the fertilizer of panic.”

Protects: Life-shrinking, agoraphobic drift, safety-behavior dependency.

Why this matters in panic: Avoidance gives short-term relief but trains long-term fear. Small, repeatable approach steps create new learning without overwhelm.

Core Anchor 5 — Body Confidence

“My body is not my enemy; sensations are data.”

Protects: Body scanning, health fear spirals, avoidance of exercise/heat/sexuality or normal arousal.

Why this matters in panic: Panic attaches to internal sensations. Practicing sensations on purpose (interoceptive exposure) builds confidence that the body can surge without danger.

Core Anchor 6 — Early Response

“Anticipatory anxiety is panic warming up—I respond early.”

Protects: Hours of dread, last-minute cancellations, over-preparing for escape.

Why this matters in panic: Intervening early prevents ‘fear rehearsal’ from priming the nervous system. Early action protects momentum and reduces avoidance learning.

Core Anchor 7 — Expansion

"I choose expansion—my life will be bigger than my fear."

Protects: Homebound patterns, restricted driving/travel, isolation.

Why this matters in panic: Panic often fears being trapped with sensations. Expansion targets distance, duration, aloneness, and visibility so freedom returns stepwise.

Core Anchor 8 — Relapse Resistance

"Waves will return; I practice the response, not perfection."

Protects: Setback catastrophizing, 'I'm back at zero,' avoidance after a spike.

Why this matters in panic: Relapse resistance prevents a single spike from becoming a slide. A re-entry plan (within 24–72 hours) protects gains.

Core Anchor 9 — Safety & Risk

"I respect real risk—without letting fear invent it."

Protects: Reassurance loops, compulsive checking, unnecessary ER/urgent-care cycles.

Why this matters in panic: Panic mimics medical emergencies. This anchor establishes a wise baseline: rule out what's needed, then practice rather than chase certainty.

Core Anchor 10 — Self-Trust

"Trust is built by evidence—I collect it on purpose."

Protects: Fragility narratives, 'I can't handle it,' low confidence after panic.

Why this matters in panic: Self-trust returns through repeated proof: 'I felt fear and stayed.' Tracking evidence strengthens capacity confidence over comfort confidence.

Core Anchor 11 — Support

"I ask for support that builds strength—not support that rescues."

Protects: Relationship strain, dependency, reassurance-driven cycles.

Why this matters in panic: Support matters, but rescue reinforces panic. Coaching support (scripts, dose-holding, celebration of practice) builds durable recovery.

Core Anchor 12 — Integration

"I keep my life open—practice is how freedom stays."

Protects: Maintenance drift, stopping practice after improvement, slow return of avoidance.

Why this matters in panic: Panic recovery is a set of skills that stay strong through use. Integration turns anchors into a flexible lifestyle, including travel and big dreams.

Appendix A
Quick Start
(If You're in a Hard Week)

If panic has been intense, your world has shrunk, or you feel "back at square one," use this quick start.

Your goal this week is not to feel great. Your goal is to stop panic from claiming more territory and to restart learning.

- Establish a simple daily plan (5 minutes)
  • Choose one anchor to practice daily (usually Anchor 3: N.A.M.E. + S.T.A.Y.).
  • Choose one small "life-open" action daily (even 5–10 minutes).
  • Choose one "rescue reduction" to practice (tiny, measurable).

- Use the 72-hour rule
  If you avoided something because of panic, re-enter a smaller version within 24–72 hours.

- Choose a minimum effective dose exposure (repeatable)
  Pick one: one aisle; one short line (60–120 seconds); one short drive; one doorway/porch step.
  Repeat before you increase.

- Reduce one safety behavior (one notch)
  Examples: check your pulse after the exposure, not during; carry water in your bag, not in your hand; delay reassurance by 10 minutes.
- Track one evidence sentence per day
  Write one line: "I felt ______ and I stayed ______."

If you can do these five steps for one week, you are back on the path.

Appendix B
Panic Signature Worksheet

Panic often feels random—until you map your personal signature.

My most common triggers (people/places/thoughts/sensations):

1) ____

2) ____

3) ____

My earliest "first sensations":

1) ____

2) ____

3) ____

My most common catastrophic story:

My most common safety behaviors / escape moves:

My top 3 avoidance areas:

1)

____

2)

____

3)

____

My top 3 values I want my life to reflect:

1)

____

2)

____

3)

____

Appendix C
The 72-Hour Re-Entry Card

Purpose: prevent panic from "claiming territory."

If I avoid, escape early, or cancel because of panic: I will re-enter a smaller version within 24–72 hours.

Example re-entry steps:

- If I left the store → return for one aisle.
- If I avoided the highway → drive to the on-ramp and back.
- If I avoided being alone → do 5 minutes alone, then check in after.

My personal re-entry plan:

Situation I avoided:

____

My smaller re-entry step:

____

When I will do it (date/time):

____

Appendix D
Interoceptive Practice Menu (Choose 1–2)

Purpose: teach your brain that sensations are tolerable and not dangerous.

Always choose a safe, reasonable intensity for you. If you have medical concerns or conditions, consult a clinician before doing sensation work.

Choose 1–2 exercises (30–90 seconds each), repeat 3–5 times per week:

- Head turns (brief dizziness): turn head side-to-side for 30 seconds.
- Stair step/fast walk (heart rate): brisk step-ups or walking in place for 60 seconds.
- Straw breathing / light air-hunger exposure (only if appropriate): breathe through a straw for 30 seconds.
- Spin in a chair (dizziness): gentle spin 10–20 seconds, then stop.
- Tense muscles (tremor sensations): tense then release shoulders/arms for 30 seconds.

- Heat sensation (if safe): hold warm mug or wear a light layer briefly, then notice heat without fixing it.

After each practice, write one line:

"I felt ______ and I stayed. It passed."

Appendix E
Reassurance & Checking Reduction Plan (Delay Ladder)

Choose ONE reassurance or checking habit to reduce:

- Pulse/oxygen checking
- Symptom Googling
- Asking "Are you sure I'm okay?"
- Calling/texting during exposure
- Repeated medical reassurance for the same pattern

My target habit:

My delay ladder (check one to start):

□ 5 minutes □ 10 minutes □ 20 minutes □ 30 minutes □ 60 minutes

□ After the planned exposure dose is complete

□ Next day unless red flags exist

During the delay, I will:

- Use N.A.M.E. + S.T.A.Y.
- Do one small valued action (not rumination).
- Repeat one script: "I can handle uncertainty for ___ minutes."

Appendix F: Supporter Guide (Coach, Not Rescuer)

Support that builds strength says: "I'm here. I believe you can handle this. Let's use your plan."

What helps (coach)

- Validate: "That's scary."
- Name the pattern: "This is panic warming up."
- Return to skills: "Use N.A.M.E. + S.T.A.Y."
- Hold the dose: "Let's stay 5 more minutes."
- Praise effort: "You stayed. That's training."

What harms (rescue)

- Repeating reassurance endlessly
- Making escape the default plan
- Doing the feared task for the person
- Forcing too-big exposure
- Arguing with symptoms

Reassurance agreement (simple)

- One reassurance statement.
- Then return to the plan.
- If asked again, repeat the same line (no new reassurance).
- Practice for a set time before asking again.

Supporter self-regulation (60 seconds)

- Feet on floor, longer exhale.
- "Coach, not rescuer."
- "Discomfort is not danger."

Appendix G
Travel & Big Dreams

My travel/big dream goal:

My top two fear profiles:

□ No escape □ No help □ Body fear □ Visibility
□ Uncertainty

My first ladder step (repeatable):

My dose (time/distance):

My travel rules

- Prepare like a person, not like panic.
- Make a plan, then stop planning.
- Reduce one safety behavior on purpose (tiny).
- Expect anxiety; don't treat it as a stop sign.

If panic hits

- Name it: "This is panic."
- Stay for the agreed dose (5–10 minutes if safe).
- Share attention (task > sensations).
- Reduce rescue (no compulsive checking/reassurance).
- Reset after: "I stayed. It passed."
- Re-enter within 72 hours if I retreated.

Appendix H
Weekly Review (15 minutes)

1) What did I practice?

2) Where did I stay open (even small)?

3) What rescue behavior did I reduce (one notch)?

4) What did panic try to convince me of—and what did I do instead?

5) Next week's plan (2 expansions, 1 aloneness step, 1 body practice):

Appendix I
Support and Crisis Resources

If you are in immediate danger, call your local emergency number.

United States

- 988 Suicide & Crisis Lifeline: call or text 988, or chat via 988lifeline.org
- Crisis Text Line: text HOME to 741741
- SAMHSA National Helpline (treatment referral): 1-800-662-HELP (4357)
- National Domestic Violence Hotline: 1-800-799-7233 or text START to 88788

Finding help

- ADAA (Anxiety & Depression Association of America): therapist directory and education
- FindTreatment.gov: treatment locator
- NAMI (National Alliance on Mental Illness): education and support groups

About the Author

Cindy H. Carr, D.Min., MACL, has spent her vocational life walking alongside people in the slow, often unseen work of formation and change. Her career has been intentionally bi-vocational, shaped by years of pastoring, business leadership, and pastoral counseling—always with a focus on helping people live with greater clarity, dignity, and wholeness.

She earned a Master of Arts in Church Leadership from Eastern Mennonite Seminary and completed her doctoral work at Liberty University. Over the years, she served multiple churches in Virginia's Shenandoah Valley in a variety of pastoral and leadership capacities.

In this season of life, Cindy's work has shifted from direct leadership into writing and education. Through her books, she helps readers implement formation-based principles she has taught throughout her career—practices centered on identity, connection, return, and steady growth without shame.

Learn more about Cindy and her work at

CindyHCarr.com

www.ingramcontent.com/pod-product-compliance
Lightning Source LLC
LaVergne TN
LVHW010659110826
845149LV00014B/3165

* 9 7 8 1 9 7 1 1 9 2 3 3 8 *